Gos

NC

INTERNATIONAL CHILDREN'S BIBLE

WORD BIBLES

WORD ENTERTAINMENT LTD
Milton Keynes, England

WORD AUSTRALIA
Nunawading, Victoria, Australia

WORD ENTERTAINMENT LTD
Vancouver, B.C., Canada

STRUIK CHRISTIAN BOOKS (PTY) LTD
Cape Town, South Africa

CAMPUS CRUSADE (ASIA) LTD
Singapore

CHRISTIAN MARKETING NEW ZEALAND LTD
Hastings, New Zealand

JENSCO LTD
Hong Kong

SALVATION BOOK CENTRE
Malaysia

INTERNATIONAL CHILDREN'S BIBLE – GOSPEL OF JOHN
New Century Version

ISBNs: 1-86024-314-2 [1-86024-315-0 (RF EDITION)]

Published by Word Publishing – a division of Word Entertainment Ltd.

Designed and produced for the publishers by Bookprint Creative Services, P.O. Box 827, BN21 3YJ, England. Printed in Great Britain.

Making Friends with Your Gospel of John

By Steve Chalke

At times the Bible can feel like the most hard-going, difficult, confusing and boring book that has ever been written.

The problem is that the Bible is very complicated.

☆ It isn't really a single book at all. The word "Bible" means "library" and that's exactly what it is – 66 books in all: 39 in the first section and 27 in the second.

☆ It was written by about 40 authors over a time period spanning more than 1000 years and it contains 750,000 words. And if that's not enough, the Old Testament was written in Hebrew and the New Testament in Greek!

So why bother? In a world where magazines, TV, radio, newspapers and other books bombard us with so many conflicting ideas about life, the Bible claims to be directly inspired by God himself – it's the creator's message to his world. If that's true it means that the Bible is in a completely different league from any other advice you can find. If the Bible is God's guidebook to life it makes sense to take it very, very seriously.

So, how do you make friends with the Bible and get the most out of reading it? Here are the ten do's and don'ts that have helped me.

1. Do use a modern translation. It's very important that you read a version which captures the depth of the original language at the same time as expressing its truth in a clear up to date way. That's where the *International Children's Bible* scores.

2. Don't rush – read slowly. Think about what you are reading. Quality comes before quantity. Read it more than once. You'll find that you'll notice all sorts of things you missed first time round. Remember that it's better to understand one verse than read a whole chapter and forget the lot!

3. Do pray first. Ask God to speak to you. You might just pray, "Help me, God, to discover you and your will as I read my Bible." After you've finished reading it pray and talk to God about the things that he has said to you or if you have found it hard to understand, be honest with him about it.

4. Don't use it as a lucky dip. Don't open it at random and expect some magic word or phrase to leap out and solve all your problems. If you do, you are almost bound to end up getting confused. And don't try and read it from cover to cover right away. As we've already said it is a big and complicated book. Like with all other guide-books the most sensible thing to do is to go to the issue you are thinking about at the time. Use one of the reading plans at the front of the Bible.

5. Do read it regularly. Just like food and exercise, "little and often" is best. If you can, set aside a short time every day to read a passage from the Bible and think it through. If your routine changes at the weekend, do something different then. Re-read what you have looked at during the week or talk it over with a friend. But remember that there is no right way to read the Bible. It's up to you to work out what suits you best.

6. Don't feel guilty if you miss a day. Why? Firstly because everyone does. So you aren't odd. Life doesn't always work out quite according to plan for anybody. Secondly, the important point isn't to have your daily dose of Bible once every 24 hours but to take in its message.

7. Do ask yourself lots of questions. It's your job to find out what it's really saying rather than inventing your own meanings. Only when you have got to grips with its original meaning can you go on to discover what it's saying to you now.

8. Don't be put off when you have a boring week or more! It happens to everyone and you are probably gaining far more than you realise – though of course that will be easier to see looking back than at the time. The secret is to be disciplined and just keep on going.

9. Do read it responsibly. Having a time when you read the Bible each day isn't an end in itself, it is only a means to an end – understanding more about Jesus Christ, your Lord and friend, boss and brother. The biggest question isn't how much we have read but about how much we have done about what we have read. Once having heard what God is saying about something we have a responsibility to act on it or to ignore it.

10. Don't be worried if you don't understand something. If you come across a difficult passage or anything that confuses you, get help. If you have a Bible commentary, concordance or Bible dictionary, check it out there. If you can't solve it ask your minister or a friend – someone that you trust to help you understand it.

Gospel of John

Christ Comes to the World

1 Before the world began, there was the Word.[1] The
Word was with God, and the Word was God. 2He was
with God in the beginning. 3All things were made
through him. Nothing was made without him. 4In him
there was life. That life was light for the people of the
world. 5The Light shines in the darkness. And the dark-
ness has not overpowered the Light.

6There was a man named John[2] who was sent by God.
7He came to tell people about the Light. Through him
all people could hear about the Light and believe. 8John
was not the Light, but he came to tell people about the
Light. 9The true Light was coming into the world. The
true Light gives light to all.

10The Word was in the world. The world was made
through him, but the world did not know him. 11He came
to the world that was his own. But his own people did
not accept him. 12But some people did accept him. They
believed in him. To them he gave the right to become
children of God. 13They did not become his children in
the human way. They were not born because of the
desire or wish of some man. They were born of God.

14 The Word became a man and lived among us. We
saw his glory – the glory that belongs to the only Son of
the Father. The Word was full of grace and truth. 15 John
told about him. He said, "This is the One I was talking
about. I said, 'The One who comes after me is greater
than I am. He was living before me'."

16 The Word was full of grace and truth. From him we
all received more and more blessings. 17 The law was
given through Moses, but grace and truth came through
Jesus Christ. 18 No man has ever seen God, but God the
only Son is very close to the Father.[3] And the Son has
shown us what God is like.

John Tells People About Jesus

19 The Jews in Jerusalem sent some priests and Levites to John.[2] The Jews sent them to ask, "Who are you?"

20 John spoke freely and did not refuse to answer. He said clearly, "I am not the Christ."[d]

21 So they asked him, "Then who are you? Are you Elijah?"[4]

He answered, "No, I am not Elijah."

Then they asked, "Are you the Prophet?"[5]

He answered, "No, I am not the Prophet."

22 Then they said, "Who are you? Give us an answer to tell those who sent us. What do you say about yourself?"

23 John told them in the words of the prophet Isaiah:

> "I am the voice of a man
> calling out in the desert:

'Make the road straight for the
Lord'."

Isaiah 40:3

24In the group of Jews who were sent, there were some
Pharisees.[d] 25They said to John: "You say you are not the
Christ. You say you are not Elijah or the Prophet. Then
why do you baptise people?"

26John answered, "I baptise people with water. But
there is one here with you that you don't know. 27He is
the One who comes after me. I am not good enough to
untie the strings of his sandals."

28This all happened at Bethany on the other side of
the Jordan River. This is where John was baptising
people.

29The next day John saw Jesus coming toward him.
John said, "Look, the Lamb of God.[6] He takes away the
sins of the world! 30This is the One I was talking about. I
said, 'A man will come after me, but he is greater than I
am, because he was living before me'. 31Even I did not
know who he was. But I came baptising with water so
that the people of Israel could know who he is."

32-33Then John said, "I did not know who the Christ
was. But God sent me to baptise with water. And God
told me, 'You will see the Spirit[d] come down and rest on
a man. That man is the One who will baptise with the
Holy Spirit'." John said, "I saw the Spirit come down from
heaven. The Spirit looked like a dove and rested on
him. 34I have seen this happen. So I tell people: 'He is
the Son of God'."

The First Followers of Jesus

35The next day John[2] was there again with two of his
followers. 36He saw Jesus walking by and said, "Look, the
Lamb of God!"[6]

37The two followers heard John say this. So they fol-
lowed Jesus. 38Jesus turned and saw them following him.
He asked, "What do you want?"

They said, "Rabbi, where are you staying?" ("Rabbi" means "Teacher".)

39Jesus answered, "Come with me and you will see."
So the two men went with Jesus. They saw the place where Jesus was staying and stayed there with him that day. It was then about four o'clock.

40These two men followed Jesus after they heard
about him from John. One of the men was Andrew. He
was Simon Peter's brother. 41The first thing Andrew
did was to find his brother, Simon. He said to Simon, "We have found the Messiah." ("Messiah" means "Christ".[d])

42Then Andrew took Simon to Jesus. Jesus looked at Simon and said, "You are Simon son of John. You will be called Cephas." ("Cephas" means "Peter".[7])

43The next day Jesus decided to go to Galilee. He
found Philip and said to him, "Follow me." 44Philip was
from the town of Bethsaida, where Andrew and Peter
lived. 45Philip found Nathanael and told him,
"Remember that Moses wrote in the law about a man who was coming, and the prophets[d] also wrote about him. We have found him. He is Jesus, the son of Joseph. He is from Nazareth."

46But Nathanael said to Philip, "Nazareth! Can anything good come from Nazareth?"

Philip answered, "Come and see."

47Jesus saw Nathanael coming toward him. He said, "Here is truly a person of Israel. There is nothing false in him."

48Nathanael asked, "How do you know me?"

Jesus answered, "I saw you when you were under the fig tree. That was before Philip told you about me."

49Then Nathanael said to Jesus, "Teacher, you are the Son of God. You are the King of Israel."

50Jesus said to Nathanael, "You believe in me
because I told you I saw you under the fig tree. But you
will see greater things than that!" 51And Jesus said to
them, "I tell you the truth. You will all see heaven open.
You will see 'angels of God going up and coming
down'[8] on the Son of Man."[d]

The Wedding at Cana

2 Two days later there was a wedding in the town of
Cana in Galilee. Jesus' mother was there. 2Jesus and
his followers were also invited to the wedding. 3When
all the wine was gone, Jesus' mother said to him, "They
have no more wine."

4Jesus answered, "Dear woman, why come to me? My time has not yet come."

5His mother said to the servants, "Do whatever he tells you to do."

6In that place there were six stone water jars. The Jews used jars like these in their washing ceremony.[9] Each jar held about 100 litres.

7Jesus said to the servants, "Fill the jars with water."
So they filled the jars to the top.
8Then he said to them, "Now take some out and give
it to the master of the feast."
So the servants took the water to the master. 9When
he tasted it, the water had become wine. He did not
know where the wine came from. But the servants who
brought the water knew. The master of the wedding
called the bridegroom 10and said to him, "People
always serve the best wine first. Later, after the guests
have been drinking a lot, they serve the cheaper wine.
But you have saved the best wine till now."
11So in Cana of Galilee, Jesus did his first miracle.[d]
There he showed his glory, and his followers believed
in him.

Jesus in the Temple

12Then Jesus went to the town of Capernaum with his
mother, brothers and his followers. They all stayed in
Capernaum for a few days. 13But it was almost time for
the Jewish Passover[d] Feast. So Jesus went to Jerusalem.
14In the Temple[d] he found men selling cattle, sheep, and
doves. He saw others sitting at tables, exchanging
money. 15Jesus made a whip out of cords. Then he
forced all these men, with the sheep and cattle, to leave
the Temple. He turned over the tables and scattered
the money of the men who were exchanging it. 16Then
he said to those who were selling pigeons, "Take these
things out of here! Don't make my Father's house a
place for buying and selling!"

17 When this happened the followers remembered
what was written in the Scriptures:[d] "My strong love for
your Temple completely controls me."[10]
18 The Jews said to Jesus, "Show us a miracle[d] for a sign.
Prove that you have the right to do these things."
19 Jesus answered, "Destroy this temple, and I will
build it again in three days."
20 The Jews answered, "Men worked 46 years to build
this Temple! Do you really believe you can build it
again in three days?"
21 (But the temple Jesus meant was his own body.
22 After Jesus was raised from death, his followers
remembered that Jesus had said this. Then they
believed the Scripture[d] and the words Jesus said.)
23 Jesus was in Jerusalem for the Passover Feast. Many
people believed in him because they saw the miracles
he did. 24 But Jesus did not trust himself to them
because he knew them all. 25 He did not need anyone to
tell him about people. Jesus knew what was in a
person's mind.

Jesus and Nicodemus

3 There was a man named Nicodemus who was one of
the Pharisees.[d] He was an important Jewish leader.
2 One night Nicodemus came to Jesus. He said, "Teacher,
we know that you are a teacher sent from God. No one
can do the miracles[d] you do, unless God is with him."
3 Jesus answered, "I tell you the truth. Unless a person
is born again, he cannot be in God's kingdom."
4 Nicodemus said, "But if a man is already old, how

can he be born again? He cannot enter his mother's
body again. So how can he be born a second time?"
5 But Jesus answered, "I tell you the truth. Unless a
person is born from water and the Spirit,[d] he cannot
enter God's kingdom. 6 A person's body is born from his
human parents. But a person's spiritual life is born from
the Spirit. 7 Don't be surprised when I tell you, 'You must
all be born again'. 8 The wind blows where it wants to go.
You hear the wind blow. But you don't know where the
wind comes from or where it is going. It is the same with
every person who is born from the Spirit."
9 Nicodemus asked, "How can all this be possible?"
10 Jesus said, "You are an important teacher in Israel.
But you still don't understand these things? 11 I tell you
the truth. We talk about what we know. We tell about
what we have seen. But you don't accept what we tell
you. 12 I have told you about things here on earth, but
you do not believe me. So certainly you will not believe
me if I tell you about the things of heaven! 13 The only
one who has ever gone up to heaven is the One who
came down from heaven – the Son of Man.[d]
14 "Moses lifted up the snake in the desert.[11] It is the
same with the Son of Man. The Son of Man must be
lifted up too. 15 Then everyone who believes in him can
have eternal life.
16 "For God loved the world so much that he gave his
only Son. God gave his Son so that whoever believes in
him may not be lost, but have eternal life. 17 God did not
send his Son into the world to judge the world guilty,
but to save the world through him. 18 He who believes in

God's Son is not judged guilty. He who does not believe
has already been judged guilty, because he has not
believed in God's only Son. 19People are judged by this
fact: I am the Light from God that has come into the
world. But men did not want light. They wanted dark-
ness because they were doing evil things. 20Everyone
who does evil hates the light. He will not come to the
light because it will show all the evil things he has done.
21But he who follows the true way comes to the light.
Then the light will show that the things he has done
were done through God."

Jesus and John the Baptist

22After this, Jesus and his followers went into the area
of Judea. There Jesus stayed with his followers and bap-
tised people. 23John was also baptising in Aenon, near
Salim, because there was plenty of water there. People
were going there to be baptised. 24(This was before John
was put into prison.)

25Some of John's followers had an argument with a Jew
about religious washing.[9] 26So they came to John and
said, "Teacher, remember the man who was with you on
the other side of the Jordan River, the one you spoke
about? He is baptising, and everyone is going to him."

27John answered, "A man can get only what God gives
him. 28You yourselves heard me say, 'I am not the
Christ.[d] I am only the one God sent to prepare the way
for him'. 29The bride belongs only to the bridegroom.
The friend who helps the bridegroom waits and listens
for him. He is glad when he hears the bridegroom's

voice. That is the same pleasure I have. And my time of
joy is now here. 30He must become greater. And I must
become less important.

The One Who Comes from Heaven

31"The One who comes from above is greater than all.
He who is from the earth belongs to the earth and talks
about things on the earth. But the One who comes from
heaven is greater than all. 32He tells what he has seen
and heard, but no one accepts what he says. 33The
person who accepts what he says has proved that God
is true. 34God sent him, and he tells the things that God
says. God gives him the Spirit[d] fully. 35The Father loves
the Son and has given him power over everything. 36He
who believes in the Son has eternal life. But he who
does not obey the Son will never have that life. God's
anger stays with him."

Jesus and a Samaritan Woman

4 "The Pharisees[d] heard that Jesus was getting and
baptising more followers than John. 2(But really Jesus
himself did not baptise people. His followers did the
baptising.) Jesus knew that the Pharisees had heard
about him. 3So he left Judea and went back to Galilee.
4On the way he had to go through the country of Samaria.
5In Samaria Jesus came to the town called Sychar. This
town is near the field that Jacob gave to his son Joseph.
6Jacob's well was there. Jesus was tired from his long
trip, so he sat down beside the well. It was about six
o'clock in the evening. 7A Samaritan[d] woman came to the

well to get some water. Jesus said to her, "Please give
me a drink." 8(This happened while Jesus' followers
were in town buying some food.)
9The woman said, "I am surprised that you ask me for
a drink. You are a Jew and I am a Samaritan." (Jews are
not friends with Samaritans.[12])
10Jesus said, "You don't know what God gives. And
you don't know who asked you for a drink. If you knew,
you would have asked me, and I would have given you
living water."
11The woman said, "Sir, where will you get that living
water? The well is very deep, and you have nothing to
get water with. 12Are you greater than Jacob, our father?
Jacob is the one who gave us this well. He drank from it
himself. Also, his sons and flocks drank from this well."
13Jesus answered, "Every person who drinks this
water will be thirsty again. 14But whoever drinks the
water I give will never be thirsty again. The water I give
will become a spring of water flowing inside him. It will
give him eternal life."
15The woman said to him, "Sir, give me this water.
Then I will never be thirsty again. And I will not have to
come back here to get more water."
16Jesus told her, "Go and get your husband and come
back here."
17The woman answered, "But I have no husband."
Jesus said to her, "You are right to say you have no
husband. 18Really you have had five husbands. But the
man you live with now is not your husband. You told the
truth."

[19]The woman said, "Sir, I can see that you are a prophet.[d] [20]Our fathers worshipped on this mountain. But you Jews say that Jerusalem is the place where people must worship."

[21]Jesus said, "Believe me, woman. The time is coming when you will not have to be in Jerusalem or on this mountain to worship the Father. [22]You Samaritans worship what you don't understand. We Jews understand what we worship. Salvation comes from the Jews. [23]The time is coming when the true worshippers will worship the Father in spirit and truth. That time is now here. And these are the kinds of worshippers the Father wants. [24]God is spirit. Those who worship God must worship in spirit and truth."

[25]The woman said, "I know that the Messiah is coming." (Messiah is the One called Christ.[d]) "When the Messiah comes, he will explain everything to us."

[26]Then Jesus said, "He is talking to you now. I am he."

[27]Just then his followers came back from town. They were surprised because they saw Jesus talking with a woman. But none of them asked, "What do you want?" or "Why are you talking with her?"

[28]Then the woman left her water jar and went back to town. She said to the people, [29] "A man told me everything I have ever done. Come and see him. Perhaps he is the Christ!" [30]So the people left the town and went to see Jesus.

[31]While the woman was away, the followers were begging him, "Teacher, eat something!"

[32]But Jesus answered, "I have food to eat that you know nothing about."

33So the followers asked themselves, "Has somebody already brought Jesus some food?"

34Jesus said, "My food is to do what the One who sent me wants me to do. My food is to finish the work that he gave me to do. 35You say, 'Four more months to wait before we gather the grain'. But I tell you, open your eyes. Look at the fields that are ready for harvesting now. 36Even now, the one who harvests the crop is being paid. He is gathering crops for eternal life. So now the one who plants can be happy along with the one who harvests. 37It is true when we say, 'One person plants, but another harvests the crop'. 38I sent you to harvest a crop that you did not work for. Others did the work, and you get the profit from their work."[13]

39Many of the Samaritans in that town believed in Jesus. They believed because of what the woman said: "He told me everything I have ever done." 40The Samaritans came to Jesus and begged him to stay with them. So he stayed there two days. 41Many more believed because of the things he said.

42They said to the woman, "First we believed in Jesus because of what you told us. But now we believe because we heard him ourselves. We know that this man really is the Saviour of the world."

Jesus Heals an Officer's Son

43Two days later, Jesus left and went to Galilee. 44(Jesus had said before that a prophet[d] is not respected in his own country.) 45When Jesus arrived in Galilee, the people there welcomed him. They had had seen all the things he did at the Passover[d] Feast in Jerusalem. They had been at the Passover Feast, too.

46Jesus went to visit Cana in Galilee again. This is where Jesus had changed the water into wine. One of the king's important officers lived in the city of Capernaum. This man's son was sick. 47The man heard that Jesus had come from Judea and was now in Galilee. He went to Jesus and begged him to come to Capernaum and heal his son. His son was almost dead. 48Jesus said to him, "You people must see signs and miracles[d] before you will believe in me."

49The officer said, "Sir, come before my child dies."

50Jesus answered, "Go. Your son will live."

The man believed what Jesus told him and went home. 51On the way the man's servants came and met him. They told him, "Your son is well."

52The man asked, "What time did my son begin to get well?"

They answered, "It was about one o'clock yesterday when the fever left him."

53The father knew that one o'clock was the exact time that Jesus had said, "Your son will live." So the man and all the people of his house believed in Jesus.

54That was the second miracle that Jesus did after coming from Judea to Galilee.

Jesus Heals a Man at a Pool

5 Later Jesus went to Jerusalem for a special Jewish feast. 2In Jerusalem there is a pool with five covered porches. In the Jewish language[14] it is called

Bethesda.[15] This pool is near the Sheep Gate. 3Many
sick people were lying on the porches beside the pool.
Some were blind, some were crippled, and some were
paralysed.[16] 5There was a man lying there who had
been sick for 38 years. 6Jesus saw the man and knew that
he had been sick for a very long time. So Jesus asked
him, "Do you want to be well?"

7The sick man answered, "Sir, there is no one to help
me get into the pool when the water starts moving. I try
to be the first one into the water. But when I try,
someone else always goes in before I can."

8Then Jesus said, "Stand up. Pick up your mat and
walk." 9And immediately the man was well. He picked
up his mat and began to walk.

The day all this happened was a Sabbath[d] day. 10So
the Jews said to the man who had been healed, "Today
is the Sabbath. It is against our law for you to carry your
mat on the Sabbath day."

11But he answered, "The man who made me well told
me, 'Pick up your mat and walk'."

12Then they asked him, "Who is the man who told you
to pick up your mat and walk?"

13But the man who had been healed did not know
who it was. There were many people in that place, and
Jesus had left.

14Later, Jesus found the man at the Temple.[d] Jesus
said to him, "See, you are well now. But stop sinning or
something worse may happen to you!"

15Then the man left and went back to the Jews. He told
them that Jesus was the one who had made him well.

16Jesus was doing this on the Sabbath day. So the Jews
began to do bad things to him. 17But Jesus said to them,
"My Father never stops working. And so I work, too."

18This made the Jews try harder to kill him. They said,
"First Jesus was breaking the law about the Sabbath day.
Then he said that God is his own Father! He is making
himself equal with God!"

Jesus Has God's Authority

19But Jesus said, "I tell you the truth. The Son can do
nothing alone. The Son does only what he sees his
Father doing. The Son does whatever the Father does.
20The Father loves the Son, and the Father shows the
Son all the things he himself does. But the Father will
show the Son greater things than this to do. Then you
will all be amazed. 21The Father raises the dead and
gives them life. In the same way, the Son gives life to
those he wants to. 22Also, the Father judges no one. But
the Father has given the Son power to do all the
judging. 23God did this so that all people will respect
the Son the same way they respect the Father. He who
does not respect the Son does not respect the Father.
The Father is the One who sent the Son.

24"I tell you the truth. Whoever hears what I say and
believes in the One who sent me has eternal life. He will
not be judged guilty. He has already left death and has
entered into life. 25I tell you the truth. The time is
coming and is already here when the dead will hear the
voice of the Son of God. And those who hear will have
life. 26Life comes from the Father himself. So the Father

has allowed the Son to give life. 27And the Father has given the Son the power to judge because he is the Son of Man.[d] 28Don't be surprised at this. A time is coming when all who are dead and in their graves will hear his voice. 29Then they will come out of their graves. Those who did good will rise and have life for ever. But those who did evil will rise to be judged guilty.

Jesus Is God's Son

30"I can do nothing alone. I judge only the way I am told, so my judgement is right. I don't try to please myself. I try to please the One who sent me.

31"If I tell people about myself, then they will not accept what I say about myself. 32But there is another who tells about me. And I know that the things he says about me are true.

33"You have sent men to John.[2] And he has told you about the truth. 34But I don't need a man to tell about me. I tell you this so that you can be saved. 35John was like a burning and shining lamp. And you were happy to enjoy his light for a while.

36"But I have a proof about myself that is greater than that of John. The things I do are my proof. These are the things my Father gave me to do. They show that the Father sent me. 37And the Father who sent me has given proof about me himself. You have never heard his voice. You have never seen what he looks like. 38His teaching does not live in you because you don't believe in the One that the Father sent. 39You carefully study the Scriptures[d] because you think that they give you eternal

life. Those are the same Scriptures that tell about me!
[40]But you refuse to come to me to have that life.
[41]"I don't want praise from men. [42]But I know you – I
know that you don't have God's love in you. [43]I have
come from my Father – I speak for him. But you don't
accept me. But when another person comes, speaking
only for himself, you will accept him. [44]You like to have
praise from each other. But you never try to get the
praise that comes from the only God. So how can you
believe? [45] Don't think that I will stand before the Father
and say that you are wrong. Moses is the one who says
that you are wrong. And he is the one that you hoped
would save you. [46]If you really believed Moses, you
would believe me because Moses wrote about me.
[47]But you don't believe what Moses wrote. So how can
you believe what I say?"

More than 5,000 People Fed

6 After this, Jesus went across Lake Galilee (or, Lake
Tiberias). [2]Many people followed him because they
saw the miracles[d] he did to heal the sick. [3]Jesus went up
on a hill and there sat down with his followers. [4]It was
almost the time for the Jewish Passover[d] Feast.
[5]Jesus looked up and saw a large crowd coming toward
him. He said to Philip, "Where can we buy bread for all
these people to eat?" [6](Jesus asked Philip this question
to test him. Jesus already knew what he planned to do.)
[7]Philip answered, "We would all have to work a month
to buy enough bread for each person here to have only
a little piece."

8Another follower there was Andrew. He was Simon
Peter's brother. Andrew said, 9"Here is a boy with five
loaves of barley bread and two little fish. But that is not
enough for so many people."

10Jesus said, "Tell the people to sit down." This was a
very grassy place. There were about 5,000 men who sat
down there. 11Then Jesus took the loaves of bread. He
thanked God for the bread and gave it to the people
who were sitting there. He did the same with the fish.
He gave them as much as they wanted.

12They all had enough to eat. When they had finished,
Jesus said to his followers, "Gather the pieces of fish and
bread that were not eaten. Don't waste anything." 13So
they gathered up the pieces that were left. They filled
12 large baskets with the pieces that were left of the five
barley loaves.

14The people saw this miracle that Jesus did. They
said, "He must truly be the Prophet[5] who is coming into
the world."

15Jesus knew that the people planned to come and
take him by force and make him their king. So he left
and went into the hills alone.

Jesus Walks on the Water

16That evening Jesus' followers went down to Lake
Galilee. 17It was dark now and Jesus had not yet come to
them. The followers got into a boat and started across
the lake to Capernaum. 18By now a strong wind was
blowing, and the waves on the lake were getting bigger.
19They rowed the boat about four or five kilometres.

Then they saw Jesus walking on the water, coming
toward the boat. The followers were afraid. 20But Jesus
said to them, "Don't be afraid. It is I." 21Then they were
glad to take him into the boat. At once the boat came to
land at the place where they wanted to go.

The People Seek Jesus

22The next day came. Some people had stayed on the
other side of the lake. They knew that Jesus had not
gone in the boat with his followers but that they had left
without him. And they knew that only one boat had
been there. 23But then some boats came from Tiberias.
They landed near the place where the people had
eaten the bread after the Lord had given thanks. 24The
people saw that Jesus and his followers were not there
now. So they got into boats and went to Capernaum.
They wanted to find Jesus.

Jesus, the Bread of Life

25The people found Jesus on the other side of the
lake. They asked him, "Teacher, when did you come
here?"

26Jesus answered, "Are you looking for me because
you saw me do miracles?[d] No! I tell you the truth. You
are looking for me because you ate the bread and were
satisfied. 27Earthly food spoils and ruins. So don't work
to get that kind of food. But work to get the food that
stays good always and gives you eternal life. The Son of
Man[d] will give you that food. God the Father has shown
that he is with the Son of Man."

28 The people asked Jesus, "What are the things God
wants us to do?"
29 Jesus answered, "The work God wants you to do is
this: to believe in the One that God sent."
30 So the people asked, "What miracle will you do? If
we can see a miracle, then we will believe you. What will
you do? 31 Our fathers ate the manna[d] in the desert. This
is written in the Scriptures:[d] 'God gave them bread from
heaven to eat'."[17]
32 Jesus said, "I tell you the truth. Moses was not the
one who gave you bread from heaven. But my Father
gives you the true bread from heaven. 33 God's bread is
the One who comes down from heaven and gives life to
the world."
34 The people said, "Sir, give us this bread always."
35 Then Jesus said, "I am the bread that gives life. He
who comes to me will never be hungry. He who believes
in me will never be thirsty. 36 But as I told you before, you
have seen me, and still you don't believe. 37 The Father
gives me my people. Every one of them will come to
me, and I will always accept them. 38 I came down from
heaven to do what God wants me to do. I did not come
to do what I want to do. 39 I must not lose even one of
those that God has given me, but I must raise them up
on the last day. This is what the One who sent me wants
me to do. 40 Everyone who sees the Son and believes in
him has eternal life. I will raise him up on the last day.
This is what my Father wants."
41 The Jews began to complain about Jesus. They com-
plained because he said, "I am the bread that comes

down from heaven." 42The Jews said, "This is Jesus. We know his father and mother. He is only Joseph's son. How can he say, 'I came down from heaven'?"

43But Jesus answered, "Stop complaining to each other. 44The Father is the One who sent me. No one can come to me unless the Father draws him to me. And I will raise him up on the last day. 45It is written in the prophets,[d] 'God will teach all the people'.[18] Everyone who listens to the Father and learns from him comes to me. 46No one has seen the Father except the One who is from God. Only he has seen the Father. 47I tell you the truth. He who believes has eternal life. 48I am the bread that gives life. 49Your ancestors ate the manna in the desert. But still they died. 50Here is the bread that comes down from heaven. If anyone eats this bread, he will never die. 51I am the living bread that came down from heaven. If anyone eats this bread, he will live for ever. This bread is my flesh. I will give my flesh so that the people in the world may have life."

52Then the Jews began to argue among themselves. They said, "How can this man give us his flesh to eat?"

53Jesus said, "I tell you the truth. You must eat the flesh of the Son of Man. And you must drink his blood. If you don't do this, then you won't have real life in you. 54He who eats my flesh and drinks my blood has eternal life. I will raise him up on the last day. 55My flesh is true food. My blood is true drink. 56Whoever eats my flesh and drinks my blood lives in me, and I live in him. 57The Father sent me. The Father lives, and I live because of the Father. So he who eats me will live because of me.

58I am not like the bread our ancestors ate. They ate that
bread, but still they died. I am the bread that came
down from heaven. He who eats this bread will live for
ever." 59Jesus said all these things while he was teaching
in the synagogue[d] in Capernaum.

The Words of Eternal Life

60The followers of Jesus heard this. Many of them said,
"This teaching is hard. Who can accept it?"

61Jesus knew that his followers were complaining
about this. So he said, "Does this teaching bother you?
62If so will it also bother you to see the Son of Man[d] going
back to the place where he came from? 63It is not the
flesh that gives a person life. It is the spirit that gives
life. The words I told you are spirit, and so they give life.
64But some of you don't believe." (Jesus knew who did
not believe. He knew this from the beginning. And he
knew who would turn against him.) 65Jesus said, "That is
the reason I said, 'If the Father does not let a person
come to me, then he cannot come'."

66After Jesus said this, many of his followers left him.
They stopped following him.

67Jesus asked the 12 followers, "Do you want to leave,
too?"

68Simon Peter answered Jesus, "Lord, where would
we go? You have the words that give eternal life. 69We
believe in you. We know that you are the Holy One from
God."

70Then Jesus answered, "I chose all 12 of you. But one
of you is a devil."

71Jesus was talking about Judas, the son of Simon
Iscariot. Judas was one of the 12. But later he was going
to turn against Jesus.

Jesus and His Brothers

7 After this, Jesus travelled around Galilee. He did not
want to travel in Judea, because the Jews there
wanted to kill him. 2It was time for the Jewish Feast[d] of
Shelters. 3So Jesus' brothers said to him, "You should
leave here and go to Judea. Then your followers there
can see the miracles[d] you do. 4Anyone who wants to be
well known does not hide what he does. If you are doing
these things, show yourself to the world." 5(Even Jesus'
brothers did not believe in him.)

6Jesus said to his brothers, "The right time for me has
not yet come. But any time is right for you. 7The world
cannot hate you. But it hates me, because I tell about
the evil things it does. 8So you go to the feast. I will not
go now. The right time for me has not yet come." 9After
saying this, Jesus stayed in Galilee.

10So Jesus' brothers left to go to the feast. When they
had gone, Jesus went, too. But he did not let people see
him. 11At the feast the Jews were looking for him. They
said, "Where is that man?"

12There was a large crowd of people there. Many of
them were whispering to each other about Jesus. Some
said, "He is a good man."

Others said, "No, he fools the people." 13But no one
was brave enough to talk about Jesus openly. They were
afraid of the Jews.

Jesus Teaches at the Feast

14 The feast was about half over. Then Jesus went to
the Temple[d] and began to teach. 15 The Jews were
amazed. They said, "This man has never studied in
school. How did he learn so much?"

16 Jesus answered, "The things I teach are not my own.
My teaching comes from him who sent me. 17 If anyone
chooses to do what God wants, then he will know that
my teaching comes from God. He will know that this
teaching is not my own. 18 He who teaches his own ideas
is trying to get honour for himself. But he who tries to
bring honour to the one who sent him – that person
speaks the truth. There is nothing false in him. 19 Moses
gave you the law,[19] but none of you obey that law. Why
are you trying to kill me?"

20 The people answered, "A demon[d] has come into
you. We are not trying to kill you."

21 Jesus said to them, "I did one miracle,[d] and you are all
amazed. 22 Moses gave you the law about circumcision.[d]
(But really Moses did not give you circumcision.
Circumcision came from our ancestors.) And yet you cir-
cumcise a baby on a Sabbath[d] day. 23 This shows that a baby
can be circumcised on a Sabbath day to obey the law of
Moses. So why are you angry at me for healing a person's
whole body on the Sabbath day? 24 Stop judging by the
way things look! Be fair, and judge by what is really right."

Is Jesus the Christ?

25 Then some of the people who lived in Jerusalem
said, "This is the man they are trying to kill. 26 But he is

teaching where everyone can see and hear him. And no
one is trying to stop him. Perhaps the leaders have
decided that he really is the Christ.[d] 27But we know
where this man is from. And when the real Christ comes,
no one will know where he comes from."
28Jesus was still teaching in the Temple.[d] He cried out,
"Yes, you know me, and you know where I am from. But
I have not come by my own authority. I was sent by the
One who is true. You don't know him. 29But I know him.
I am from him, and he sent me."
30When Jesus said this, the people tried to take him.
But no one was able to touch him. It was not yet the right
time. 31But many of the people believed in Jesus. They
said, "When the Christ comes, will he do more miracles[d]
than this man has done?"

Some Leaders Try to Arrest Jesus

32The Pharisees[d] heard the crowd whispering these
things about Jesus. So the leading priests and the
Pharisees sent some Temple[d] guards to arrest him.
33Then Jesus said, "I will be with you a little while longer.
Then I will go back to the One who sent me. 34You will
look for me, but you will not find me. And you cannot
come where I am."
35The Jews said to each other, "Where will this man go
so we cannot find him? Will he go to the Greek cities
where our people live? Will he teach the Greek people
there? 36This man says, 'You will look for me but you will
not find me'. He also says, 'You cannot come where I
am'. What does this mean?"

Jesus Talks About the Spirit

37The last day of the feast came. It was the most
important day. On that day Jesus stood up and said
in a loud voice, "If anyone is thirsty, let him come to
me and drink. 38If a person believes in me, rivers of
living water will flow out from his heart. This is what
the Scripture[d] says." 39Jesus was talking about the
Holy Spirit.[d] The Spirit had not yet been given
because Jesus had not yet been raised to glory. But
later, those who believed in Jesus would receive the
Spirit.

The People Argue About Jesus

40The people heard these things that Jesus said.
Some of them said, "This man really is the Prophet."[5]
41Others said, "He is the Christ."[d] Still others said,
"The Christ will not come from Galilee. 42The Scripture[d]
says that the Christ will come from David's family. And
the Scripture says that the Christ will come from
Bethlehem, the town where David lived." 43So the
people did not agree with each other about Jesus.
44Some of them wanted to arrest him, but no one was
able to touch him.

The Leaders Won't Believe

45The Temple[d] guards went back to the leading
priests and the Pharisees.[d] The priests and the
Pharisees asked, "Why didn't you bring Jesus?"
46The Temple guards answered, "The things he says
are greater than the words of any man!"

47The Pharisees answered, "So Jesus has fooled you
too! 48Have any of the leaders or the Pharisees believed
in him? No! 49But those people, who know nothing
about the law, are under God's curse!"
50But Nicodemus was there in that group. He was the
one who had gone to see Jesus before.[20] Nicodemus
said, 51"Our law does not judge a man without hearing
him. We cannot judge him until we know what he has
done."
52They answered, "Are you from Galilee too? Study
the Scriptures.[d] You will learn that no prophet[d] comes
from Galilee."
53And everyone left and went home.[21]

The Woman Caught in Adultery

8 Jesus went to the Mount of Olives.[d] 2But early in the
morning he went back to the Temple.[d] All the
people came to Jesus, and he sat and taught them. 3The
teachers of the law and the Pharisees[d] brought a woman
there. She had been caught in adultery.[d] They forced
the woman to stand before the people. 4They said to
Jesus, "Teacher, this woman was caught having sexual
relations with a man who is not her husband. 5The law of
Moses commands that we kill with stones every woman
who does this. What do you say we should do?" 6They
were asking this to trick Jesus so that they could have
some charge against him.

But Jesus knelt down and started writing on the
ground with his finger. 7They continued to ask Jesus
their question. So he stood up and said, "Is there

anyone here who has never sinned? The person without
sin can throw the first stone at this woman." 8Then Jesus
knelt down again and wrote on the ground.
9Those who heard Jesus began to leave one by one.
The older men left first, and then the others. Jesus was
left there alone with the woman. She was standing
before him. 10Jesus stood up again and asked her,
"Woman, all of those people have gone. Has no one
judged you guilty?"
11She answered, "No one has judged me, sir."
Then Jesus said, "So I don't judge you either. You may
go now, but don't sin again."

Jesus Is the Light of the World

12Later, Jesus talked to the people again. He said, "I
am the light of the world. The person who follows me
will never live in darkness. He will have the light that
gives life."
13But the Pharisees[d] said to Jesus, "When you talk
about yourself, you are the only one to say these things
are true. We cannot accept these things you say."
14Jesus answered, "Yes, I am saying these things
about myself, but they are true. I know where I came
from. And I know where I am going. You don't know
where I came from or where I am going. 15You judge me
the way you would judge any man. I don't judge anyone.
16But if I judge, my judging is true. When I judge, I am
not alone. The Father who sent me is with me. 17Your
own law says that when two witnesses say the same
thing, then you must accept what they say. 18I am one of

the witnesses who speaks about myself. And the Father
who sent me is my other witness."
19They asked, "Where is your father?"
Jesus answered, "You don't know me or my Father.
But if you knew me, then you would know my Father,
too." 20Jesus said these things while he was teaching in
the Temple.[d] He was near the place where the money
that the people give is kept. But no one arrested him.
The right time for Jesus had not yet come.

The People Misunderstand Jesus

21Again, Jesus said to the people, "I will leave you.
You will look for me, but you will die in your sins. You
cannot come where I am going."
22So the Jews asked, "Will Jesus kill himself? Is that
why he said, 'You cannot come where I am going'?"
23But Jesus said, "You people are from here below,
but I am from above. You belong to this world, but I
don't belong to this world. 24So I told you that you would
die in your sins. Yes, you will die in your sins if you don't
believe that I am he."
25They asked, "Then who are you?"
Jesus answered, "I am what I have told you from the
beginning. 26I have many things to say about you and to
judge you for. But I tell people only the things I have
heard from the One who sent me. And he speaks the
truth."
27The people did not understand that Jesus was
talking to them about the Father. 28So Jesus said to
them, "You will lift up the Son of Man.[d] Then you will

know that I am he. You will know that these things I do
are not by my own authority. You will know that I say
only what the Father has taught me. 29The One who sent
me is with me. I always do what is pleasing to him. So he
has not left me alone." 30While Jesus was saying these
things, many people believed in him.

Freedom from Sin

31So Jesus said to the Jews who believed in him, "If
you continue to obey my teaching, you are truly my fol-
lowers. 32Then you will know the truth. And the truth will
make you free."

33The Jews answered, "We are Abraham's children.
And we have never been slaves. So why do you say that
we will be free?"

34Jesus answered, "I tell you the truth. Everyone who
lives in sin is a slave to sin. 35A slave does not stay with
a family for ever, but a son belongs to the family for ever.
36So if the Son makes you free, then you will be truly
free. 37I know you are Abraham's children. But you want
to kill me because you don't accept my teaching. 38I am
telling you what my Father has shown me. But you do
what your father has told you."

39They answered, "Our father is Abraham."

Jesus said, "If you were really Abraham's children, you
would do the things that Abraham did. 40I am a man who
has told you the truth which I heard from God. But you
are trying to kill me. Abraham did nothing like that. 41So
you are doing the things that your own father did."

But the Jews said, "We are not like children who never

knew who their father was. God is our Father. He is the
only Father we have."
42Jesus said to them, "If God were really your Father,
you would love me. I came from God and now I am here.
I did not come by my own authority. God sent me. 43You
don't understand what I say because you cannot accept
my teaching. 44Your father is the devil. You belong to
him and want to do what he wants. He was a murderer
from the beginning. He was against the truth, for there
is no truth in him. He is a liar, and he is like the lies he
tells. He is the father of lies. 45But I speak the truth. That
is why you don't believe me. 46Can any of you prove that
I am guilty of sin? If I am telling the truth, why don't you
believe me? 47He who belongs to God accepts what
God says. But you don't accept what God says, because
you don't belong to God."

Jesus and Abraham

48The Jews answered, "We say you are a Samaritan![d]
We say a demon[d] has come into you. Are we not right?"
49Jesus answered, "I have no demon in me. I give
honour to my Father, but you dishonour me. 50I am
not trying to get honour for myself. There is One who
wants this honour for me, and he is the judge. 51I tell
you the truth. If anyone obeys my teaching, he will
never die."
52The Jews said to Jesus, "Now we know that you have
a demon in you! Even Abraham and the prophets[d] died.
But you say, 'Whoever obeys my teaching will never
die'. 53Do you think that you are greater than our father

Abraham? Abraham died. And the prophets died, too.
Who do you think you are?"
54 Jesus answered, "If I give honour to myself, that
honour is worth nothing. The One who gives me honour
is my Father. And you say that he is your God. 55 But you
don't really know him. I know him. If I said I did not know
him, then I would be a liar as you are liars. But I do know
him, and I obey what he says. 56 Your father Abraham was
very happy that he would see my day. He saw that day
and was glad."
57 The Jews said to him, "What? You have seen
Abraham! You are not even 50 years old!"
58 Jesus answered, "I tell you the truth. Before
Abraham was born, I am!" 59 When Jesus said this, the
people picked up stones to throw at him. But Jesus hid
himself, and then he left the Temple.[d]

Jesus Heals a Man Born Blind

9 As Jesus was walking along, he saw a man who had
been born blind. 2 His followers asked him, "Teacher,
whose sin caused this man to be born blind – his own
sin or his parents' sin?"
3 Jesus answered, "It is not this man's sin or his
parents' sin that caused him be blind. This man was
born blind so that God's power could be shown in him.
4 While it is day time, we must continue doing the work
of the One who sent me. The night is coming. And no
one can work at night. 5 While I am in the world, I am the
light of the world."
6 After Jesus said this, he spat on the ground and

made some mud with it. He put the mud on the man's
eyes. [7]Then he told the man, "Go and wash in the Pool
of Siloam." (Siloam means Sent.) So the man went to the
pool. He washed and came back. And he was able to
see.

[8]Some people had seen this man begging before.
They and the man's neighbours said, "Look! Is this the
same man who always sits and begs?"

[9]Some said, "Yes! He is the one." But others said, "No,
he's not the same man. He only looks like him."

So the man himself said, "I am the man."

[10]They asked, "What happened? How did you get
your sight?"

[11]He answered, "The man named Jesus made some
mud and put it on my eyes. Then he told me to go to
Siloam and wash. So I went and washed and came back
seeing."

[12]They asked him, "Where is this man?"

The man answered, "I don't know."

Pharisees Question the Healing

[13]Then the people took to the Pharisees[d] the man
who had been blind. [14]The day Jesus had made mud
and healed his eyes was a Sabbath[d] day. [15]So now the
Pharisees asked the man, "How did you get your sight?"

He answered, "He put mud on my eyes. I washed, and
now I can see."

[16]Some of the Pharisees were saying, "This man does
not keep the Sabbath day. He is not from God!"

Others said, "But a man who is a sinner can't do miracles[d] like these." So they could not agree with each other.

17They asked the man again, "What do you say about him? It was your eyes he opened."

The man answered, "He is a prophet."[d]

18The Jews did not believe that he had been blind and could now see again. So they sent for the man's parents 19and asked them, "Is this your son? You say that he was born blind. Then how does he see now?"

20His parents answered, "We know that this is our son, and we know that he was born blind. 21But we don't know how he can see now. We don't know who opened his eyes. Ask him. He is old enough to answer for himself." 22His parents said this because they were afraid of the Jews. The Jews had already decided that anyone who said that Jesus was the Christ[d] would be put out of the synagogue.[d] 23That is why his parents said, "He is old enough. Ask him."

24So for the second time, the Jewish leaders called the man who had been blind. They said, "You should give God the glory by telling the truth. We know that this man is a sinner."

25He answered, "I don't know if he is a sinner. But one thing I do know. I was blind, and now I can see."

26The Jewish leaders asked, "What did he do to you? How did he make you see again?"

27He answered, "I have already told you that. But you would not listen to me. Why do you want to hear it again? Do you want to become his followers, too?"

[28]Then they insulted him and said, "You are his follower. We are followers of Moses. [29]We know that God spoke to Moses. But we don't even know where this man comes from!"

[30]The man answered, "This is a very strange thing. You don't know where he comes from, and yet he opened my eyes. [31]We all know that God does not listen to sinners. But God listens to anyone who worships and obeys him. [32]Nobody has ever heard of anyone giving sight to a man born blind. [33]If this man was not from God, he could do nothing."

[34]They answered, "You were born full of sin! Are you trying to teach us?" And they threw the man out.

Spiritual Blindness

[35]Jesus heard that they had thrown him out. So Jesus found him and said, "Do you believe in the Son of Man?"[d]

[36]He asked, "Who is the Son of Man, sir? Tell me, so I can believe in him!"

[37]Jesus said to him, "You have already seen him. The Son of Man is the one talking with you now."

[38]He said, "Yes, Lord, I believe!" Then the man bowed and worshipped Jesus.

[39]Jesus said, "I came into this world that the world could be judged. I came so that the blind[22] could see and so that those who see will become blind."

[40]Some of the Pharisees[d] were near Jesus. When they heard him say this, they asked, "What? Are you saying that we are blind, too?"

41Jesus said, "If you were really blind, you would not
be guilty of sin. But now that you say you can see, your
guilt remains."

The Shepherd and His Sheep

10 Jesus said, "I tell you the truth. The man who
does not enter the sheep fold by the door,
but climbs in some other way, is a thief and a robber.
2The one who enters by the door is the shepherd of
the sheep. 3The man who guards the door opens it for
him. And the sheep listen to the voice of the shep-
herd. He calls his own sheep, using their names, and
he leads them out. 4He brings all of his sheep out.
Then he goes ahead of them and leads them. They
follow him because they know his voice. 5But they will
never follow a stranger. They will run away from him
because they don't know his voice." 6Jesus told the
people this story, but they did not understand what it
meant.

Jesus Is the Good Shepherd

7So Jesus said again, "I tell you the truth. I am the door
for the sheep. 8All the people who came before me were
thieves and robbers. The sheep did not listen to them.
9I am the door. The person who enters through me will
be saved. He will be able to come in and go out and find
pasture. 10A thief comes to steal and kill and destroy.
But I came to give life – life in all its fullness.

11"I am the good shepherd. The good shepherd gives
his life for the sheep. 12The worker who is paid to keep

the sheep is different from the shepherd who owns
them. So when the worker sees a wolf coming, he runs
away and leaves the sheep alone. Then the wolf attacks
the sheep and scatters them. [13]The man runs away
because he is only a paid worker. He does not really
care for the sheep.

[14–15]"I am the good shepherd. I know my sheep, as the
Father knows me. And my sheep know me, as I know the
Father. I give my life for the sheep. [16]I have other sheep
that are not in this flock here. I must bring them also.
They will listen to my voice, and there will be one flock
and one shepherd. [17]The Father loves me because I
give my life. I give my life so that I can take it back again.
[18]No one takes it away from me. I give my own life freely.
I have the right to give my life, and I have the right to
take it back. This is what my Father commanded me to
do."

[19]Again the Jews did not agree with each other
because of these words Jesus said. [20]Many of them said,
"A demon[d] has come into him and made him mad. Why
listen to him?"

[21]But others said, "A man who is mad with a demon
does not say things like this. Can a demon open the
eyes of the blind?"

[22]The time came for the Feast[d] of Dedication at
Jerusalem. This was during the winter. [23]Jesus was
walking in the Temple[d] in Solomon's Porch.[d] [24]The Jews
gathered around him and said, "How long will you make
us wonder about you? If you are the Christ,[d] then tell us
plainly."

Jesus Is the Son of God

25 Jesus answered, "I have told you already, but you
did not believe. I do miracles[d] in my Father's name.
Those miracles show who I am. 26 But you don't believe
because you are not my sheep. 27 My sheep listen to my
voice. I know them, and they follow me. 28 I give them
eternal life, and they will never die. And no person can
steal them out of my hand. 29 My Father gave my sheep
to me. He is greater than all, and no person can steal my
sheep out of my Father's hand. 30 The Father and I are
one."

31 Again the Jews picked up stones to kill Jesus. 32 But
Jesus said to them, "I have done many good works from
the Father. Which of these good works are you killing me
for?"

33 The Jews answered, "We are not killing you for any
good work you did. But you say things that are against
God. You are only a man, but you say you are the same
as God!"

34 Jesus answered, "It is written in your law that God
said, 'I have said you are gods!'[23] 35 This scripture[d]
called those people gods, the people who received
God's message. And Scripture is always true. 36 So why
do you say that I speak against God because I said, 'I am
God's Son'? I am the one God chose and sent into the
world. 37 If I don't do what my Father does, then don't
believe me. 38 But if I do what my Father does, even
though you don't believe in me, believe what I do. Then
you will know and understand that the Father is in me
and I am in the Father."

39The Jews tried to take Jesus again, but he escaped
from them.
40Then Jesus went back across the Jordan River to the
place where John[2] had first baptised. Jesus stayed
there, 41and many people came to him. They said, "John
never did a miracle. But everything John said about this
man is true." 42And in that place many believed in Jesus.

The Death of Lazarus

11 There was a man named Lazarus who was sick. He
lived in the town of Bethany, where Mary and her
sister Martha lived. 2Mary is the woman who later put
perfume on the Lord and wiped his feet with her hair.
Mary's brother was Lazarus, the man who was now sick.
3So Mary and Martha sent someone to tell Jesus, "Lord,
the one you love is sick."
4When Jesus heard this he said, "This sickness will not
end in death. It is for the glory of God. This has happened
to bring glory to the Son of God." 5Jesus loved Martha and
her sister and Lazarus. 6But when he heard that Lazarus
was sick, he stayed where he was for two more days. 7Then
Jesus said to his followers, "Let us go back to Judea."
8The followers said, "But Teacher, the Jews there tried
to kill you with stones. That was only a short time ago.
Now you want to go back there?"
9Jesus answered, "Are there not 12 hours in the day?
If anyone walks in the daylight, he will not stumble
because he can see by this world's light. 10But if anyone
walks at night he stumbles because there is no light to
help him see."

11After Jesus said this, he added, "Our friend Lazarus
has fallen asleep. But I am going there to wake him."
12The followers said, "But Lord, if he can sleep, he will
get well."
13Jesus meant that Lazarus was dead. But Jesus' fol-
lowers thought that he meant Lazarus was really sleep-
ing. 14So then Jesus said plainly, "Lazarus is dead. 15And
I am glad for your sakes that I was not there so that you
may believe. But let us go to him now."
16Then Thomas (the one called Didymus) said to the
other followers, "Let us go, too. We will die with him."

Jesus in Bethany

17Jesus arrived in Bethany. There he learned that
Lazarus had already been dead and in the tomb for four
days. 18Bethany was about three kilometres from
Jerusalem. 19Many Jews had come there to comfort
Martha and Mary about their brother.
20Martha heard that Jesus was coming, and she went
out to meet him. But Mary stayed at home. 21Martha
said to Jesus, "Lord, if you had been here, my brother
would not have died. 22But I know that even now God
will give you anything you ask."
23Jesus said, "Your brother will rise and live again."
24Martha answered, "I know that he will rise and live
again in the resurrection[24] on the last day."
25Jesus said to her, "I am the resurrection and the life.
He who believes in me will have life even if he dies.
26And he who lives and believes in me will never die.
Martha, do you believe this?"

27Martha answered, "Yes, Lord. I believe that you are
the Christ,[d] the Son of God. You are the One who was
coming to the world."

Jesus Cries

28After Martha said this, she went back to her sister
Mary. She talked to Mary alone. Martha said, "The Teacher
is here and he is asking for you." 29When Mary heard this,
she got up quickly and went to Jesus. 30Jesus had not yet
come into the town. He was still at the place where Martha
had met him. 31The Jews were with Mary in the house,
comforting her. They saw Mary stand and leave quickly.
They followed her, thinking that she was going to the tomb
to cry there. 32But Mary went to the place where Jesus was.
When she saw him, she fell at his feet and said, "Lord, if
you had been here, my brother would not have died."

33Jesus saw that Mary was crying and that the Jews
who came with her were crying, too. Jesus felt very sad
in his heart and was deeply troubled. 34He asked,
"Where did you bury him?"

"Come and see, Lord," they said.

35Jesus cried.

36So the Jews said, "See how much he loved him."

37But some of them said, "If Jesus healed the eyes of
the blind man, why didn't he keep Lazarus from dying?"

Jesus Raises Lazarus

38Again Jesus felt very sad in his heart. He came to the
tomb. The tomb was a cave with a large stone covering
the entrance. 39Jesus said, "Move the stone away."

Martha said, "But, Lord, it has been four days since he
died. There will be a bad smell." Martha was the sister
of the dead man.
40Then Jesus said to her, "Didn't I tell you that if you
believed, you would see the glory of God?"
41So they moved the stone away from the entrance.
Then Jesus looked up and said, "Father, I thank you that
you heard me. 42I know that you always hear me. But I
said these things because of the people here around
me. I want them to believe that you sent me." 43After
Jesus said this, he cried out in a loud voice, "Lazarus,
come out!" 44The dead man came out. His hands and
feet were wrapped with pieces of cloth, and he had a
cloth around his face.
Jesus said to them, "Take the cloth off him and let him
go."

The Leaders Plan to Kill Jesus

45There were many Jews who had come to visit Mary.
They saw what Jesus did. And many of them believed in
him. 46But some of the Jews went to the Pharisees.[d] They
told the Pharisees what Jesus had done. 47Then the
leading priests and Pharisees called a meeting of the
Jewish council. They asked, "What should we do? This
man is doing many miracles.[d] 48If we let him continue
doing these things, everyone will believe in him. Then
the Romans will come and take away our Temple[d] and
our nation."
49One of the men there was Caiaphas. He was the high
priest that year. Caiaphas said, "You people know

nothing! [50]It is better for one man to die for the people
than for the whole nation to be destroyed. But you don't
realise this."
[51]Caiaphas did not think of this himself. He was high
priest that year. So he was really prophesying[d] that Jesus
would die for the Jewish nation [52]and for God's scattered
children. This would bring them all together and make
them one.
[53]That day the Jewish leaders started planning to kill
Jesus. [54]So Jesus no longer travelled openly among the
Jews. He left there and went to a place near the desert.
He went to a town called Ephraim and stayed there with
his followers.
[55]It was almost time for the Jewish Passover[d] Feast.
Many from the country went up to Jerusalem before the
Passover. They went to do the special things to make
themselves pure. [56]The people looked for Jesus. They
stood in the Temple and were asking each other, "Is he
coming to the Feast? What do you think?" [57]But the
leading priests and the Pharisees had given orders
about Jesus. They said that if anyone knew where Jesus
was, he must tell them. Then they could arrest Jesus.

Jesus with Friends in Bethany

12 Six days before the Passover[d] Feast, Jesus went
to Bethany, where Lazarus lived. (Lazarus is the
man Jesus raised from death.) [2]There they had a dinner
for Jesus. Martha served the food. Lazarus was one of
the people eating with Jesus. [3]Mary brought in half a
litre of very expensive perfume made from pure nard.[d]

She poured the perfume on Jesus' feet, and then she
wiped his feet with her hair. And the sweet smell from
the perfume filled the whole house.

4Judas Iscariot, one of Jesus' followers, was there.
(He was the one who would later turn against Jesus.)
Judas said, 5"This perfume was worth 300 silver
coins.[25] It should have been sold and the money
given to the poor." 6But Judas did not really care about
the poor. He said this because he was a thief. He was
the one who kept the money box, and he often stole
money from it.

7Jesus answered, "Leave her alone. It was right for her
to save this perfume for today – the day for me to be
prepared for burial. 8The poor will always be with you,
but you will not always have me."

The Plot Against Lazarus

9A large crowd of Jews heard that Jesus was in
Bethany. So they went there to see not only Jesus but
also Lazarus. Lazarus was the one Jesus raised from
death. 10So the leading priests made plans to kill
Lazarus, too. 11Because of Lazarus many Jews were
leaving them and believing in Jesus.

Jesus Enters Jerusalem

12The next day a great crowd in Jerusalem heard that
Jesus was coming there. These were the people who
had come to the Passover[d] Feast. 13They took branches
of palm trees and went out to meet Jesus. They
shouted,

"Praise[26] God!
God bless the One who comes in the name of the Lord!
God bless the King of Israel!"

Psalm 118: 25–26

14Jesus found a colt and sat on it. This was as the
Scripture[d] says,

15"Don't be afraid, people of Jerusalem!
Your king is coming.
He is sitting on the colt of a donkey."

Zechariah 9:9

16The followers of Jesus did not understand this at first. But after Jesus was raised to glory, they remembered that this had been written about him. And they remembered that they had done these things to him.

People Tell About Jesus

17There had been many people with Jesus when he raised Lazarus from death and told him to come out of the tomb. Now they were telling others about what Jesus
did. 18Many people went out to meet Jesus, because
they had heard about this miracle.[d] 19So the Pharisees[d]
said to each other, "You can see that nothing is going right for us. Look! The whole world is following him."

Jesus Talks About His Death

20There were some Greek people, too, who came to
Jerusalem to worship at the Passover[d] Feast. 21They

went to Philip. (Philip was from Bethsaida, in Galilee.)
They said, "Sir, we would like to see Jesus." 22Philip told
Andrew. Then Andrew and Philip told Jesus.

23Jesus said to them, "The time has come for the Son
of Man[d] to receive his glory. 24I tell you the truth. A grain
of wheat must fall to the ground and die. Then it makes
many seeds. But if it never dies, it remains only a single
seed. 25The person who loves his life will give up true
life. But the person who hates his life in this world will
keep true life for ever. 26Whoever serves me must follow
me. Then my servant will be with me everywhere I am.
My Father will honour anyone who serves me.

27"Now I am very troubled. What should I say? Should
I say, 'Father, save me from this time'? No, I came to this
time so that I could suffer. 28Father, bring glory to your
name!"

Then a voice came from heaven, "I have brought glory
to it, and I will do it again."

29The crowd standing there heard the voice. They
said it was thunder.

But others said, "An angel has spoken to him."

30Jesus said, "That voice was for you, not for me.
31Now is the time for the world to be judged. Now the
ruler of this world will be thrown down. 32I will be lifted
up from the earth. And when this happens, I will draw
all people toward me." 33Jesus said this to show how he
would die.

34The crowd said, "We have heard from the law that
the Christ[d] will live for ever. So why do you say, 'The Son
of Man must be lifted up'? Who is this 'Son of Man'?"

35 Then Jesus said, "The light will be with you for a
little longer. So walk while you have the light. Then the
darkness will not catch you. He who walks in the dark-
ness does not know where he is going. 36 So believe in
the light while you still have it. Then you will become
sons of light." When Jesus had said this, he left and hid
himself from them.

Some Don't Believe in Jesus

37 Though Jesus had done many miracles[d] before the
people, they still did not believe in him. 38 This was to make
clear the full meaning of what Isaiah the prophet[d] said:

"Lord, who believed the things we told them?
Who has seen the Lord's power?"

Isaiah 53:1

39 This is why the people could not believe: Isaiah also
said,

40 "He has blinded their eyes.
He has closed their minds.
This is so that they will not see with their eyes
nor understand in their minds.
This is so they will not
come back to me and be forgiven."

Isaiah 6:10

41 Isaiah said this because he saw Jesus' glory and
spoke about him.

42But many people believed in Jesus, even many of
the Jewish leaders. But because of the Pharisees,[d] they
did not say that they believed in him. They were afraid
that they would be put out of the synagogue.[d] 43They
loved praise from men more than praise from God.

44Then Jesus cried out, "He who believes in me is
really believing in the One who sent me. 45He who sees
me sees the One who sent me. 46I have come as light
into the world. I came so that whoever believes in me
would not stay in darkness.

47"If anyone hears my words and does not obey them,
I do not judge him. For I did not come to judge the
world, but to save the world. 48There is a judge for the
one who refuses to believe in me and does not accept
my words. The word I have taught will be his judge on
the last day. 49The things I taught were not from myself.
The Father who sent me told me what to say and what
to teach. 50And I know that eternal life comes from what
the Father commands. So whatever I say is what the
Father told me to say."

Jesus Washes His Followers' Feet

13 It was almost time for the Jewish Passover[d] Feast.
Jesus knew that it was time for him to leave this
world and go back to the Father. He had always loved
those who were his own in the world, and he loved them
all the way to the end.

2Jesus and his followers were at the evening meal.
The devil had already persuaded Judas Iscariot to turn
against Jesus. (Judas was the son of Simon.) 3Jesus

knew that the Father had given him power over every-
thing. He also knew that he had come from God and
was going back to God. 4So during the meal Jesus stood
up and took off his outer clothing. Taking a towel, he
wrapped it around his waist. 5Then he poured water
into a bowl and began to wash the followers' feet. He
dried them with the towel that was wrapped around
him.

6Jesus came to Simon Peter. But Peter said to Jesus,
"Lord, are you going to wash my feet?"

7Jesus answered, "You don't understand what I am
doing now. But you will understand later."

8Peter said, "No! You will never wash my feet."

Jesus answered, "If I don't wash your feet, then you
are not one of my people."

9Simon Peter answered, "Lord, after you wash my
feet, wash my hands and my head, too!"

10Jesus said, "After a person has had a bath, his whole
body is clean. He needs only to wash his feet. And you
men are clean,[d] but not all of you." 11Jesus knew who
would turn against him. That is why Jesus said, "Not all
of you are clean."

12When he had finished washing their feet, he put on
his clothes and sat down again. Jesus asked, "Do you
understand what I have just done for you? 13You call me
'Teacher' and 'Lord'. And this is right, because that is
what I am. 14I, your Lord and Teacher, have washed your
feet. So you also should wash each other's feet. 15I did
this as an example for you. So you should do as I have
done for you. 16I tell you the truth. A servant is not

greater than his master. A messenger is not greater than
the one who sent him. [17]If you know these things, you
will be happy if you do them.
[18]"I am not talking about all of you. I know those I have
chosen. But what the Scripture[d] said must happen: 'The
man who ate at my table has now turned against me'.[27]
[19]I am telling you this now before it happens. Then when
it happens you will believe that I am he. [20]I tell you the
truth. Whoever accepts anyone I send also accepts me.
And whoever accepts me also accepts the One who sent
me."

Jesus Talks About His Death

[21]After Jesus said this, he was very troubled. He said
openly, "I tell you the truth. One of you will turn against
me."
[22]The followers all looked at each other. They did not
know whom Jesus was talking about. [23]One of the fol-
lowers was sitting[28] next to Jesus. This was the follower
Jesus loved. [24]Simon Peter made signs to him to ask
Jesus who it was that he was talking about.
[25]That follower leaned closer to Jesus and asked,
"Lord, who is it that will turn against you?"
[26]Jesus answered, "I will dip this bread into the dish.
The man I give it to is the man who will turn against me."
So Jesus took a piece of bread. He dipped it and gave it
to Judas Iscariot, the son of Simon. [27]As soon as Judas
took the bread, Satan entered him. Jesus said to Judas,
"The thing that you will do – do it quickly!" [28]None of the
men at the table understood why Jesus said this to Judas.

29He was the one who kept the money box. So some of the followers thought that Jesus was telling Judas to buy what was needed for the feast. Or they thought that Jesus wanted Judas to give something to the poor.

30Judas accepted the bread Jesus gave him and immediately went out. It was night.

31When Judas was gone, Jesus said, "Now the Son of Man[d] receives his glory. And God receives glory through him. 32If God receives glory through him, then God will give glory to the Son through himself. And God will give him glory quickly."

33Jesus said, "My children, I will be with you only a little longer. You will look for me. And what I told the Jews, I tell you now: where I am going you cannot come.

34"I give you a new command: love each other. You must love each other as I have loved you. 35All people will know that you are my followers if you love each other."

Peter Will Say He Doesn't Know Jesus

36Simon Peter asked Jesus, "Lord, where are you going?"

Jesus answered, "Where I am going you cannot follow now. But you will follow later."

37Peter asked, "Lord, why can't I follow you now? I am ready to die for you!"

38Jesus answered, "Will you really die for me? I tell you the truth. Before the cock crows, you will say three times that you don't know me."

Jesus Comforts His Followers

14 Jesus said, "Don't let your hearts be troubled.
Trust in God. And trust in me. [2]There are many
rooms in my Father's house. I would not tell you this if
it were not true. I am going there to prepare a place for
you. [3]After I go and prepare a place for you, I will come
back. Then I will take you to be with me so that you may
be where I am. [4]You know the way to the place where I
am going."

[5]Thomas said to Jesus, "Lord, we don't know where
you are going. So how can we know the way?"

[6]Jesus answered, "I am the way. And I am the truth and
the life. The only way to the Father is through me. [7]If you
really knew me, then you would know my Father, too.
But now you do know him, and you have seen him."

[8]Philip said to him, "Lord, show us the Father. That is
all we need."

[9]Jesus answered, "I have been with you a long time
now. Do you still not know me, Philip? He who has seen
me has seen the Father. So why do you say, 'Show us
the Father'? [10]Don't you believe that I am in the Father
and the Father is in me? The words I say to you don't
come from me. The Father lives in me, and he is doing
his own work. [11]Believe me when I say that I am in the
Father and the Father is in me. Or believe because of
the miracles[d] I have done. [12]I tell you the truth. He who
believes in me will do the same things that I do. He will
do even greater things than these because I am going
to the Father. [13]And if you ask for anything in my name,
I will do it for you. Then the Father's glory will be shown

through the Son. 14If you ask me for anything in my name, I will do it.

The Promise of the Holy Spirit

15"If you love me, you will do the things I command. 16I will ask the Father, and he will give you another Helper.[29] He will give you this Helper to be with you for ever. 17The Helper is the Spirit[d] of truth. The world cannot accept him because it does not see him or know him. But you know him. He lives with you and he will be in you.

18"I will not leave you all alone like orphans. I will come back to you. 19In a little while the world will not see me any more, but you will see me. Because I live, you will live, too. 20On that day you will know that I am in my Father. You will know that you are in me and I am in you. 21He who knows my commands and obeys them is the one who loves me. And my Father will love him who loves me. I will love him and will show myself to him."

22Then Judas (not Judas Iscariot) said, "But, Lord, why do you plan to show yourself to us, but not to the world?"

23Jesus answered, "If anyone loves me, then he will obey my teaching. My Father will love him, and we will come to him and make our home with him. 24He who does not love me does not obey my teaching. This teaching that you hear is not really mine. It is from my Father, who sent me.

25"I have told you all these things while I am with you.

26 But the Helper will teach you everything. He will cause
you to remember all the things I told you. This Helper
is the Holy Spirit whom the Father will send in my name.
27 "I leave you peace. My peace I give you. I do not
give it to you as the world does. So don't let your hearts
be troubled. Don't be afraid. 28 You heard me say to you,
'I am going, but I am coming back to you'. If you loved
me, you should be happy that I am going back to the
Father because he is greater than I am. 29 I have told you
this now, before it happens. Then when it happens, you
will believe. 30 I will not talk with you much longer. The
ruler of this world is coming. He has no power over me.
31 But the world must know that I love the Father. So I do
exactly what the Father told me to do.

"Come now, let us go."

Jesus Is Like a Vine

15 "I am the true vine; my Father is the gardener.
2 He cuts off every branch of mine that does not
produce fruit. And he trims and cleans every branch that
produces fruit so that it will produce even more fruit.
3 You are already clean[d] because of the words I have
spoken to you. 4 Remain in me, and I will remain in you.
No branch can produce fruit alone. It must remain in the
vine. It is the same with you. You cannot produce fruit
alone. You must remain in me.

5 "I am the vine, and you are the branches. If a person
remains in me and I remain in him, then he produces
much fruit. But without me he can do nothing. 6 If anyone
does not remain in me, then he is like a branch that is

thrown away. That branch dies. People pick up dead
branches, throw them into the fire, and burn them.
7Remain in me and follow my teachings. If you do this,
then you can ask for anything you want, and it will be
given to you. 8You should produce much fruit and show
that you are my followers. This brings glory to my Father.
9I loved you as the Father loved me. Now remain in my
love. 10I have obeyed my Father's commands, and I
remain in his love. In the same way, if you obey my com-
mands, you will remain in my love. 11I have told you
these things so that you can have the same joy I have. I
want your joy to be the fullest joy.

12"This is my command: love each other as I have
loved you. 13The greatest love a person can show is to
die for his friends. 14You are my friends if you do what I
command you. 15I don't call you servants now. A servant
does not know what his master is doing. But now I call
you friends because I have made known to you every-
thing I heard from my Father. 16You did not choose me;
I chose you. And I gave you this work, to go and produce
fruit. I want you to produce fruit that will last. Then the
Father will give you anything you ask for in my name.
17This is my command: love each other.

Jesus Warns His Followers

18"If the world hates you, remember that it hated me
first. 19If you belonged to the world, then it would love
you as it loves its own. But I have chosen you out of the
world. So you don't belong to it. That is why the world
hates you. 20Remember what I told you: a servant is not

greater than his master. If people did wrong to me, they
will do wrong to you, too. And if they obeyed my teach-
ing, they will obey yours, too. 21They will do all this to
you because of me. They don't know the One who sent
me. 22If I had not come and spoken to them, they would
not be guilty of sin. But now they have no excuse for
their sin. 23He who hates me also hates my Father. 24I did
works among them that no one else has ever done. If I
had not done those works, they would not be guilty of
sin. But now they have seen what I did, and yet they
have hated both me and my Father. 25But this hap-
pened so that what is written in their law would be true:
'They hated me for no reason'.[30]

26"I will send you the Helper[29] from the Father. He is
the Spirit of truth who comes from the Father. When he
comes, he will tell about me. 27And you also must tell
people about me because you have been with me from
the beginning.

16 "I have told you these things to keep you from
giving up. 2People will put you out of their syna-
gogues.[d] Yes, the time is coming when whoever kills you
will think that he is offering service to God. 3They will do
this because they have not known the Father and they
have not known me. 4I have told you these things now.
So when the time comes, you will remember that I
warned you.

The Work of the Holy Spirit

"I did not tell you these things at the beginning,
because I was with you then. 5Now I am going back to

the One who sent me. But none of you asks me, 'Where
are you going?' 6 Your hearts are filled with sadness
because I have told you these things. 7 But I tell you the
truth. It is better for you that I go away. When I go away
I will send the Helper[29] to you. If I do not go away, then
the Helper will not come. 8 When the Helper comes, he
will prove to the people of the world the truth about sin,
about being right with God, and about judgement. 9 He
will prove to them about sin, because they don't
believe in me. 10 He will prove to them that I am right
with God, because I am going to the Father. You will not
see me any more. 11 And the Helper will prove to them
the truth about judgement, because the ruler of this
world is already judged.

12 "I have many more things to say to you, but they are
too much for you now. 13 But when the Spirit[d] of truth
comes he will lead you into all truth. He will not speak
his own words. He will speak only what he hears and will
tell you what is to come. 14 The Spirit of truth will bring
glory to me. He will take what I have to say and tell it to
you. 15 All that the Father has is mine. That is why I said
that the Spirit will take what I have to say and tell it to
you.

Sadness Will Become Happiness

16 "After a little while you will not see me. And then
after a little while you will see me again."

17 Some of the followers said to each other, "What
does Jesus mean when he says, 'After a little while you
will not see me, and then after a little while you will see

me again'? And what does he mean when he says,
'Because I am going to the Father'?" 18They also asked,
"What does he mean by 'a little while'? We don't under-
stand what he is saying."
19Jesus saw that the followers wanted to ask him
about this. So Jesus said to the followers, "Are you
asking each other what I meant when I said, 'After a little
while you will not see me. And then after a little while
you will see me again'? 20I tell you the truth. You will cry
and be sad, but the world will be happy. You will be sad,
but your sadness will become joy. 21When a woman
gives birth to a baby, she has a pain, because her time
has come. But when her baby is born, she forgets the
pain. She forgets because she is so happy that a child
has been born into the world. 22 It is the same with you.
Now you are sad. But I will see you again and you will be
happy. And no one will take away your joy. 23In that day
you will not ask me for anything. I tell you the truth. My
Father will give you anything you ask for in my name.
24You have never asked for anything in my name. Ask
and you will receive. And your joy will be the fullest joy.

Victory over the World

25"I have told you these things, using words that hide
the meaning. But the time will come when I will not use
words like that to tell you things. I will speak to you in
plain words about the Father. 26In that day you will ask
the Father for things in my name. I am saying that I will
not need to ask the Father for you. 27No! The Father
himself loves you. He loves you because you have loved

me. And he loves you because you have believed that I
came from God. 28I came from the Father into the world.
Now I am leaving the world and going back to the Father."
29Then the followers of Jesus said, "You are speaking
clearly to us now. You are not using words that are hard
to understand. 30We can see now that you know all things.
You can answer a person's question even before he asks
it. This makes us believe that you came from God."
31Jesus answered, "So now you believe? 32Listen to
me. A time is coming when you will be scattered. Each
of you will be scattered to his own home. That time is
now here. You will leave me. I will be alone. But I am
never really alone. Why? Because the Father is with me.
33"I told you these things so that you can have peace
in me. In this world you will have trouble. But be brave!
I have defeated the world!"

Jesus Prays for His Followers

17 After Jesus said these things he looked towards
heaven. Jesus prayed, "Father, the time has
come. Give glory to your Son so that the Son can give
glory to you. 2You gave the Son power over all people
so that the Son could give eternal life to all those
people you have given to him. 3And this is eternal life:
that men can know you, the only true God, and that men
can know Jesus Christ, the One you sent. 4I have finished
the work you gave me to do. I have brought you glory on
earth. 5And now, Father, give me glory with you. Give me
the glory I had with you before the world was made.
6"You gave me some men from the world. I have

shown them what you are like. Those men belonged to
you, and you gave them to me. They have obeyed your
teaching. [7]Now they know that everything you gave me
comes from you. [8]I gave these men the teachings that
you gave me. They accepted those teachings. They
know that I truly came from you. [9]I pray for them now. I
am not praying for the people in the world. But I am
praying for those men you gave me, because they are
yours. [10]All I have is yours, and all you have is mine. And
my glory is shown through these men. [11]Now I am
coming to you. I will not stay in the world now. But these
men are still in the world. Holy Father, keep them safe.
Keep them safe by the power of your name (the name
you gave me), so that they will be one, the same as you
and I are one. [12]While I was with them, I kept them safe.
I kept them safe by the power of your name – the name
you gave me. I protected them. And only one of them,
the one who is going to hell, was lost. He was lost so that
what was said in the Scripture[d] would happen.

[13]"I am coming to you now. But I pray these things
while I am still in the world. I say these things so that
these men can have my joy. I want them to have all of
my joy. [14]I have given them your teaching. And the world
has hated them. The world hated these men, because
they don't belong to the world, just as I don't belong to
the world. [15]I am not asking you to take them out of the
world. But I am asking that you keep them safe from the
Evil One. [16]They don't belong to the world, just as I don't
belong to the world. [17]Make them ready for your service
through your truth. Your teaching is truth. [18]I have sent

them into the world, just as you sent me into the world.
19 I am making myself ready to serve. I do this for them
so that they can truly be ready for your service.
20 "I pray for these men. But I am also praying for all
people who will believe in me because of the teaching
of these men. 21 Father, I pray that all people who
believe in me can be one. You are in me and I am in you.
I pray that these people can also be one in us, so that
the world will believe that you sent me. 22 I have given
these people the glory that you gave me. I gave them
this glory so that they can be one, just as you and I are
one. 23 I will be in them and you will be in me. So they
will be completely one. Then the world will know that
you sent me. And the world will know that you loved
these people just as you loved me.
24 "Father, I want those you have given me to be with
me in every place I am. I want them to see my glory. This
is the glory you gave me because you loved me before
the world was made. 25 Father, you are the One who is
good. The world does not know you, but I know you. And
these people know that you sent me. 26 I showed them
what you are like. And again I will show them what you
are like. Then they will have the same love that you
have for me. And I will live in them."

Jesus Is Arrested

18 When Jesus finished praying, he left with his followers. They went across the Kidron Valley. On the other side there was a garden of olive trees. Jesus and his followers went there.

2Judas knew where this place was, because Jesus met
there often with his followers. Judas was the one who
turned against Jesus. 3So Judas led a group of soldiers
to the garden. Judas also brought some guards from the
leading priests and the Pharisees.[d] They were carrying
torches, lanterns, and weapons.

4Jesus knew everything that would happen to him.
Jesus went out and asked, "Who is it you are looking
for?"

5The men answered, "Jesus from Nazareth."

Jesus said, "I am Jesus." (Judas, the one who turned
against Jesus, was standing there with them.) 6When
Jesus said, "I am Jesus," the men moved back and fell to
the ground.

7Jesus asked them again, "Who is it you are looking
for?"

They said, "Jesus of Nazareth."

8Jesus said, "I told you that I am he. So if you are
looking for me, then let these other men go." 9This hap-
pened so that the words Jesus said before might come
true: "I have not lost any of the men you gave me."

10Simon Peter had a sword. He took out the sword and
struck the servant of the high priest, cutting off his right
ear. (The servant's name was Malchus.) 11Jesus said to
Peter, "Put your sword back. Shall I not drink of the
cup[31] the Father has given me?"

Jesus Is Brought Before Annas

12Then the soldiers with their commander and the
Jewish guards arrested Jesus. They tied him 13and led

him first to Annas. Annas was the father-in-law of
Caiaphas, the high priest that year. 14Caiaphas was the
one who had told the Jews that it would be better if one
man died for all the people.

Peter Says He Doesn't Know Jesus

15Simon Peter and another one of Jesus' followers
went along after Jesus. This follower knew the high
priest. So he went with Jesus into the high priest's court-
yard. 16But Peter waited outside near the door. The fol-
lower who knew the high priest came back outside. He
spoke to the girl at the door and brought Peter inside.
17The girl at the door said to Peter, "Aren't you also one
of that man's followers?"

Peter answered, "No, I am not!"

18It was cold, so the servants and guards had built a
fire. They were standing around it and warming them-
selves. Peter was standing with them, warming himself.

The High Priest Questions Jesus

19The high priest asked Jesus questions about his fol-
lowers and his teaching. 20Jesus answered, "I have
spoken openly to everyone. I have always taught in syn-
agogues[d] and in the Temple,[d] where all the Jews come
together. I never said anything in secret. 21So why do
you question me? Ask the people who heard my teach-
ing. They know what I said."

22When Jesus said this, one of the guards standing
there hit him. The guard said, "Is that the way you
answer the high priest?"

23 Jesus answered him, "If I said something wrong,
then say what was wrong. But if what I said is true, why
do you hit me?"
24 Then Annas sent Jesus to Caiaphas, the high priest.
Jesus was still tied.

Peter Says Again He Doesn't Know Jesus

25 Simon Peter was standing and warming himself.
They said to him, "Aren't you one of that man's follow-
ers?"
Peter denied it and said, "No, I am not."
26 One of the servants of the high priest was there. This
servant was a relative of the man whose ear Peter had
cut off. The servant said, "Didn't I see you with him in
the garden?"
27 Again Peter said it wasn't true. Just then a cockerel
crowed.

Jesus Is Brought Before Pilate

28 Then the Jews led Jesus from Caiaphas' house to the
Roman governor's palace. It was early in the morning.
The Jews would not go inside the palace. They did not
want to make themselves unclean,[32] because they
wanted to eat the Passover[d] meal. 29 So Pilate went
outside to them. He asked, "What charges do you bring
against this man?"
30 They answered, "He is a criminal. That is why we
brought him to you."
31 Pilate said to the Jews, "Take him yourselves and
judge him by your own law."

They answered, "But we are not allowed to put
anyone to death." 32(This happened so that what Jesus
had said about how he would die would come true.)
33Then Pilate went back inside the palace. He called
Jesus to him and asked, "Are you the king of the Jews?"
34Jesus said, "Is that your own question, or did others
tell you about me?"
35Pilate answered, "I am not a Jew. It was your own
people and their leading priests who brought you
before me. What have you done wrong?"
36Jesus said, "My kingdom does not belong to this
world. If it belonged to this world, my servants would
fight so that I would not be given over to the Jews. But
my kingdom is from another place."
37Pilate said, "So you are a king!"
Jesus answered, "You say that I am a king. That is true.
I was born for this: to tell people about the truth. That is
why I came into the world. And everyone who belongs
to the truth listens to me."
38Pilate said, "What is truth?" After he said this, he
went out to the Jews again. He said to them, "I can find
nothing to charge against this man. 39But it is your
custom that I free one prisoner to you at the time of the
Passover. Do you want me to free this 'King of the
Jews'?"
40They shouted back, "No, not him! Let Barabbas go
free!" (Barabbas was a robber.)
19 Then Pilate ordered that Jesus be taken away
and whipped. 2The soldiers used some thorny
branches to make a crown. They put this crown on Jesus'

head and put a purple robe around him. 3Then they
came to Jesus many times and said, "Hail, King of the
Jews!" They hit Jesus in the face.

4Again Pilate came out and said to the Jews, "Look! I
am bringing Jesus out to you. I want you to know that I
find nothing I can charge against him." 5Then Jesus came
out, wearing the crown of thorns and the purple robe.
Pilate said to the Jews, "Here is the man!"

6When the leading priests and the Jewish guards saw
Jesus they shouted, "Kill him on a cross! Kill him on a
cross!"

But Pilate answered, "Take him and nail him to a cross yourselves. I find nothing I can charge against him."

7The Jews answered, "We have a law that says he
should die, because he said he is the Son of God."

8When Pilate heard this, he was even more afraid. 9He
went back inside the palace and asked Jesus, "Where
are you from?" But Jesus did not answer him. 10Pilate
said, "You refuse to speak to me? Don't you know that I
have power to set you free and power to have you killed
on a cross?"

11Jesus answered, "The only power you have over me
is the power given to you by God. The man who gave me
to you is guilty of a greater sin."

12After this, Pilate tried to let Jesus go free. But the
Jews cried out, "Anyone who makes himself king is
against Caesar. If you let this man go free, you are not
Caesar's friend."

13Pilate heard what the Jews were saying. So he
brought Jesus out to the place called The Stone

Pavement. (In the Jewish language[14] the name is
Gabbatha.) Pilate sat down on the judge's seat there.
14It was about six o'clock in the morning on Preparation[d]
Day of Passover[d] week. Pilate said to the Jews, "Here is
your king!"
15The Jews shouted, "Take him away! Take him away!
Kill him on a cross!"

Pilate asked them, "Do you want me to kill your king
on a cross?"

The leading priests answered, "The only king we have
is Caesar!"
16So Pilate gave Jesus to them to be killed on a cross.

Jesus Is Killed on a Cross

The soldiers took charge of Jesus. 17Carrying his own
cross, Jesus went out to a place called The Place of the
Skull. (In the Jewish language[14] this place is called
Golgotha.) 18There they nailed Jesus to the cross. They
also put two other men on crosses, one on each side of
Jesus with Jesus in the middle. 19Pilate wrote a sign and
put it on the cross. It read: "JESUS OF NAZARETH, THE KING OF
THE JEWS." 20The sign was written in the Jewish language,
in Latin, and in Greek. Many of the Jews read the sign,
because this place where they killed Jesus was near the
city. 21The leading Jewish priests said to Pilate, "Don't
write, 'The King of the Jews'. But write, 'This man said, I
am the King of the Jews'."
22Pilate answered, "What I have written, I have
written!"
23After the soldiers nailed Jesus to the cross, they

took his clothes. They divided them into four parts.
Each soldier got one part. They also took his long shirt.
It was all one piece of cloth, woven from top to bottom.
24So the soldiers said to each other, "We should not tear
this into parts. We should throw lots[d] to see who will get
it." This happened to give full meaning to the Scripture:[d]

> "They divided my clothes among them.
> And they threw lots[d] for my clothing."
>
> *Psalm* 22:18

So the soldiers did this.
25Jesus' mother stood near his cross. His mother's sister
was also standing there, with Mary the wife of Clopas,
and Mary Magdalene. 26Jesus saw his mother. He also
saw the follower he loved standing there. He said to his
mother, "Dear woman, here is your son." 27Then he said
to the follower, "Here is your mother." From that time
on, this follower took her to live in his home.

Jesus Dies

28After this, Jesus knew that everything had been
done. To make the Scripture[d] come true, he said, "I am
thirsty."[33] 29There was a jar full of vinegar there, so the
soldiers soaked a sponge in it. Then they put the
sponge on a branch of a hyssop plant and lifted it to
Jesus' mouth. 30Jesus tasted the vinegar. Then he said,
"It is finished." He bowed his head and died.

31This day was Preparation[d] Day. The next day was a
special Sabbath[d] day. The Jews did not want the bodies

to stay on the cross on the Sabbath day. So they asked
Pilate to order that the legs of the men be broken[34] and
the bodies be taken away. 32So the soldiers came and
broke the legs of the first man on the cross beside Jesus.
Then they broke the legs of the man on the other cross
beside Jesus. 33But when the soldiers came to Jesus,
they saw that he was already dead. So they did not
break his legs, 34but one of the soldiers stuck his spear
into Jesus' side. At once blood and water came out.
35(The one who saw this happen has told about it. The
things he says are true. He knows that he tells the truth.
He told about it so that you also can believe.) 36These
things happened to make the Scripture come true: "Not
one of his bones will be broken."[35] 37And another
Scripture said, "They will look at the one they have
stabbed."[36]

Jesus is Buried

38Later, a man named Joseph from Arimathea asked
Pilate if he could take the body of Jesus. (Joseph was a
secret follower of Jesus, because he was afraid of the
Jews.) Pilate gave his permission. So Joseph came and
took Jesus' body away. 39Nicodemus went with Joseph.
Nicodemus was the man who earlier had come to Jesus
at night. He brought about 35 kilograms of spices. This
was a mixture of myrrh[d] and aloes.[d] 40These two men
took Jesus' body and wrapped it with the spices in
pieces of linen cloth. (This is how the Jews bury people.)
41In the place where Jesus was killed, there was a
garden. In the garden was a new tomb where no one had

ever been buried. 42The men laid Jesus in that tomb because it was near, and the Jews were preparing to start their Sabbath[d] day.

Jesus' Tomb Is Empty

20 Early on the first day of the week, Mary Magdalene went to the tomb. It was still dark. Mary saw that the large stone had been moved away from the tomb. 2So Mary ran to Simon Peter and the other followcr (the one Jesus loved). Mary said, "They have taken the Lord out of the tomb. We don't know where they have put him."

3So Peter and the other follower started for the tomb. 4They were both running, but the other follower ran faster than Peter. So the other follower reached the tomb first. 5He bent down and looked in. He saw the strips of linen cloth lying there, but he did not go in. 6Then following him came Simon Peter. He went into the tomb and saw the strips of linen lying there. 7He also saw the cloth that had been around Jesus' head. The cloth was folded up and laid in a different place from the strips of linen. 8Then the other follower, who had reached the tomb first, also went in. He saw and believed. 9(These followers did not yet understand from the Scriptures[d] that Jesus must rise from death.)

Jesus Appears to Mary Magdalene

10Then the followers went back home. 11But Mary stood outside the tomb, crying. While she was still crying, she bent down and looked inside the tomb.

12She saw two angels dressed in white. They were sitting
where Jesus' body had been, one at the head and one
at the feet.
13They asked her, "Woman, why are you crying?"
She answered, "They have taken away my Lord. I
don't know where they have put him." 14When Mary said
this, she turned around and saw Jesus standing there.
But she did not know that it was Jesus.
15Jesus asked her, "Woman, why are you crying?
Whom are you looking for?"
Mary thought he was the gardener. So she said to him,
"Did you take him away, sir? Tell me where you put him,
and I will get him."
16Jesus said to her, "Mary."
Mary turned toward Jesus and said in the Jewish lan-
guage,[14] "Rabboni." (This means Teacher.)
17Jesus said to her, "Don't hold me. I have not yet
gone up to the Father. But go to my brothers and tell
them this: 'I am going back to my Father and your
Father. I am going back to my God and your God'."
18Mary Magdalene went and said to the followers, "I
have seen the Lord!" And she told them what Jesus had
said to her.

Jesus Appears to His Followers

19It was the first day of the week. That evening the
followers were together. The doors were locked,
because they were afraid of the Jews. Then Jesus came
and stood among them. He said, "Peace be with you!"
20After he said this, he showed them his hands and his

side. The followers were very happy when they saw the
Lord.
[21]Then Jesus said again, "Peace be with you! As the
Father sent me, I now send you." [22]After he said this, he
breathed on them and said, "Receive the Holy Spirit.[d]
[23]If you forgive anyone his sins, they are forgiven. If you
don't forgive them, they are not forgiven."

Jesus Appears to Thomas

[24]Thomas (called Didymus) was not with the followers
when Jesus came. Thomas was one of the 12. [25]The other
followers told Thomas, "We have seen the Lord."
But Thomas said, "I will not believe it until I see the nail
marks in his hands. And I will not believe until I put my
finger where the nails were and put my hand into his side."
[26]A week later the followers were in the house again.
Thomas was with them. The doors were locked, but
Jesus came in and stood among them. He said, "Peace
be with you!" [27]Then he said to Thomas, "Put your finger
here. Look at my hands. Put your hand here in my side.
Stop doubting and believe."
[28]Thomas said to him, "My Lord and my God!"
[29]Then Jesus told him, "You believe because you see
me. Those who believe without seeing me will be truly
happy."

Why John Wrote This Book

[30]Jesus did many other miracles[d] in front of his fol-
lowers that are not written in this book. [31]But these are
written so that you can believe that Jesus is the Christ,[d]

the Son of God. Then, by believing, you can have life
through his name.

Jesus Appears to Seven Followers

21 Later, Jesus showed himself to his followers by
Lake Galilee.[37] This is how it happened. 2Some
of the followers were together. They were Simon Peter,
Thomas (called Didymus), Nathanael from Cana in
Galilee, the two sons of Zebedee, and two other follow-
ers. 3Simon Peter said, "I am going out to fish."

The other followers said, "We will go with you." So
they went out and got into the boat. They fished that
night but caught nothing.

4Early the next morning Jesus stood on the shore. But
the followers did not know that it was Jesus. 5Then he
said to them, "Friends, have you caught any fish?"

They answered, "No".

6He said, "Throw your net into the water on the right
side of the boat, and you will find some." So they did
this. They caught so many fish that they could not pull
the net back into the boat.

7The follower whom Jesus loved said to Peter, "It is
the Lord!" When Peter heard him say this, he wrapped
his coat around himself. (Peter had taken his clothes
off.) Then he jumped into the water. 8The other follow-
ers went to shore in the boat, dragging the net full of
fish. They were not very far from shore, only about 100
metres. 9When the followers stepped out of the boat
and onto the shore, they saw a fire of hot coals. There
were fish on the fire, and there was bread.

10 Then Jesus said, "Bring some of the fish that you
caught."
11 Simon Peter went into the boat and pulled the net
to the shore. It was full of big fish. There were 153. Even
though there were so many, the net did not tear. 12 Jesus
said to them, "Come and eat." None of the followers
dared ask him, "Who are you?" They knew it was the
Lord. 13 Jesus came and took the bread and gave it to
them. He also gave them the fish.
14 This was now the third time that Jesus showed
himself to his followers after he was raised from death.

Jesus Talks to Peter

15 When they had finished eating, Jesus said to Simon
Peter, "Simon, son of John, do you love me more than
these?"

He answered, "Yes, Lord, you know that I love you."

Jesus said, "Take care of my lambs."

16 Again Jesus said, "Simon, son of John, do you love
me?"

He answered, "Yes, Lord, you know that I love you."

Jesus said, "Take care of my sheep."

17 A third time he said, "Simon, son of John, do you
love me?"

Peter was hurt because Jesus asked him the third time, "Do you love me?" Peter said, "Lord, you know everything. You know that I love you!"

He said to him, "Take care of my sheep. 18 I tell you the
truth. When you were younger, you tied your own belt
and went where you wanted. But when you are old, you

will put out your hands and someone else will tie them.
They will take you where you don't want to go." 19(Jesus
said this to show how Peter would die to give glory to
God.) Then Jesus said to Peter, "Follow me!"

20Peter turned and saw that the follower Jesus loved
was walking behind them. (This was the follower who
had leaned against Jesus at the supper and had said,
"Lord, who will turn against you?") 21When Peter saw
him behind them he asked Jesus, "Lord, what about
him?"

22Jesus answered, "Perhaps I want him to live until I
come back. That should not be important to you. You
follow me!"

23So a story spread among the brothers that this follower would not die. But Jesus did not say that he would not die. He only said, "Perhaps I want him to live until I come back. That should not be important to you."

24That follower is the one who is telling these things. He is the one who has now written them down. We know that what he says is true.

25There are many other things that Jesus did. If every one of them were written down, I think the whole world would not be big enough for all the books that would be written.

Notes

[1] The Greek word is "logos", meaning any kind of communication. It could be translated "message". Here, it means Christ. Christ was the way God told people about himself.

[2] John the Baptist, who preached to people about Christ's coming (Matthew 3, Luke 3).

[3] This could be translated, "but the only God is very close to the Father." Also, some Greek copies say, "but the only Son is very close to the Father."

[4] A man who spoke for God. He lived hundreds of years before Christ.

[5] They probably meant the prophet that God told Moses he would send (Deuteronomy 18:15-19).

[6] Name for Jesus. Jesus is like the lambs that were offered as a sacrifice to God.

[7] The Greek name "Peter", like the Aramaic name "Cephas", means "rock".

[8] These words are from Genesis 28:12.

[9] The Jews washed themselves in special ways before eating, before worshipping in the Temple, and at other special times.

[10] Quotation from Psalm 69:9.

[11] The people of Israel were dying from snake bites. God told Moses to put a brass snake on a pole. The people who looked at the snake were healed (Numbers 21:4-9).

[12] This can also be translated "Jews don't use things that Samaritans have used".

[13] As a farmer sends workers to harvest grain, Jesus sends his followers out to bring people to God.

[14] Aramaic, the language of the Jews in the first century.

[15] Also called Bethsaida or Bethzatha, a pool of water north of the Temple in Jerusalem.

[16] Some Greek copies add "and they waited for the water to move". A few later copies add verse 4: "Sometimes an angel of the Lord came down to the pool

and stirred up the water. After the angel did this, the first person to go into the pool was healed of any sickness he had."

[17] Quotation from Psalm 78:24.

[18] Quotation from Isaiah 54:13.

[19] Moses gave God's people the law that God gave him on Mount Sinai (Exodus 34:29-32).

[20] The story about Nicodemus going and talking to Jesus is in John 3:1-21.

[21] Some early Greek manuscripts do not contain 7:53–8:11.

[22] Jesus is talking about people who are spiritually blind, not physically blind.

[23] Quotation from Psalm 82:6.

[24] Being raised from death to live again.

[25] One coin, a denarius, was the average pay for one day's work.

[26] Literally, "Hosanna", a Hebrew word used at first in praying to God for help, but at this time it was probably a shout of joy used in praising God or his Messiah.

[27] Quotation from Psalm 41:9.

[28] Literally, "lying". The people of that time ate lying down and leaning on one arm.

[29] "Counsellor", or "Comforter". Jesus is talking about the Holy Spirit.

[30] These words could be from Psalm 35:19 or Psalm 69:4.

[31] Jesus is talking about the bad things that will happen to him. Accepting these things will be very hard, like drinking a cup of something that tastes very bitter.

[32] Going into a non-Jewish place would make them unfit to eat the Passover Feast, according to Jewish law.

[33] Read Psalms 22:15, 69:21.

[34] The breaking of the men's bones would make them die sooner.

[35] Quotation from Psalm 34:20. The idea is from Exodus 12:46; Numbers 9:12.

[36] Quotation from Zechariah 12:10.

[37] Literally, "Sea of Tiberias".

Dictionary

Adultery (ah-DUL-ter-ee) is breaking a marriage promise by having sexual relations with someone other than your husband or wife. (Exodus 20:14; Mark 10:11,12; John 8:3–5)

Aloes (AL-ohs) were oils from sweet-smelling sap of certain trees. They were used for perfume, medicine and to prepare bodies for burial. (Numbers 24:6; John 19:39)

Christ (KRYST) means "anointed (or chosen) one" in Greek. In Hebrew the word is "Messiah". Jesus is the Christ. He was chosen by God to save people from their sins. (Mark 8:29; 14:61,62; Luke 23:2; Acts 2:36; 17:3; 18:28)

Circumcision (SIR-kum-SIH-zhun) This means to cut off the foreskin of the male sex organ. Each Jewish baby boy was circumcised on the eighth day after he was born. This act was done as a sign of the agreement God had made with his people, the Jews. Because of this, the Jews sometimes are called "the circumcision" and non-Jews are called "the uncircumcision". (Leviticus 12:3; John 7:22; Acts 7:8)

Clean is used to describe the state of a person, animal or action that is pleasing to God. God called some animals clean and said they could be eaten. People who had not touched or eaten anything God said was unclean were called clean. Or, if they did not have a disease that made them unclean, they were called clean. They could live and serve God normally. (Genesis 7:2; Leviticus 20:25; Deuteronomy 14:3–20).

Demon (DEE-mun) was an evil spirit from the devil. Sometimes a demon lived in a person. But Jesus has more power than demons and could make them come out of people. (Deuteronomy 32:17; Psalm 106:37; Matthew 12:22; Luke 8:26–39)

Feast of Dedication was an eight-day celebration for the Jews. It was a way of being thankful that the Temple had been cleansed again. This was done in 164 B.C. after the Greeks had spoiled and ruined it. The celebration is called Hanukkah today by the Jews. (John 10:22)

Feast of Shelters is also called the Feast of Booths or Feast of Tabernacles. The people gathered fruit and lived in tent-like shelters for a week. This feast reminded them of how God had taken care of them when the Israelites left Egypt and lived in tents in the wilderness. (Exodus 23:14–17; Deuteronomy 16:13–17)

Holy Spirit (HO-lee SPIH-rit) is one of the three persons of God. The other two persons are God the Father and God the Son (Jesus). The Holy Spirit helped the apostles do miracles. He led men to write God's word. The Holy Spirit lives in Christians today. He is also called the Spirit of Christ, the Spirit of God, and the Comforter. (Genesis 1:2; John 3:5–8; 16:13; Acts 2:1–4; 5:32; Romans 5:5; 8:9–16; 2 Peter 1:20,21)

Lots were sticks, stones or pieces of bone thrown like dice to decide something. Often God controlled the result of the lots to let the people know what he wanted them to do. (Numbers 26:55,56; Proverbs 18:18; Jonah 1:7; Luke 1:9; 23:34; Acts 1:26)

Manna (MAN-ah) means "what is it?" It was the white, sweet-tasting food God gave the people of Israel in the wilderness. It appeared on the ground during the night so they could gather it in the morning. (Exodus 16:13–35; Numbers 11:7–9; Joshua 5:12; Hebrews 9:4)

Miracle (MYR-ih-k'l) is a Latin word that means "wonderful thing". It is a great event which can be done only by God's help. Miracles are special signs to show God's power. In the Old Testament God used miracles to rescue his people. Jesus did miracles to prove that he was God's Son. The Bible tells us of many miracles. The sick were healed, the blind were given sight, the crippled were able to walk and people could speak languages they had never studied. Sometimes people were even brought back to life after they had died. The best miracle was Jesus' coming back to life after he was killed on the cross. (Nehemiah 9:17; Psalm 77:11,14; Matthew 28:5–7; Luke 23:8; John 2:1–11; 3:2; 20:30,31; Acts 4:16–22; 8:13)

Mount of Olives is a hill covered with olive trees near Jerusalem. The garden of Gethsemane is on one side of the Mount of Olives. Jesus was praying there when the Roman soldiers came to arrest him. Some of the same olive trees that were in the garden when Jesus was on earth may still be there today. (2 Samuel 15:30; Luke 22:39–52; Acts 1:12)

Myrrh (MUR) was a sweet-smelling liquid taken from certain trees and shrubs. It was used as a perfume and as a pain reliever. It was one of the gifts the wise men gave Jesus when he was born. (Genesis 37:25; 43:11; Proverbs 7:17; Matthew 2:11; Mark 15:23; John 19:39)

Nard was an expensive perfume. It was expensive because it had to be imported from India. (Song of Solomon 4:13; Mark 14:3; John 12:3)

Passover Feast (PASS-o-ver FEEST) was an important holy day for the Jews in the spring of each year. They ate a special meal on this day to remind them that God had freed them from being slaves in Egypt. Jesus was killed at Passover time. (Exodus 12:27; Numbers 9; Joshua 5:10; Matthew 26:2,17–19)

Pharisees (FA-rih-seez) means "the separate people". They were a Jewish religious group who followed the religious laws and customs very strictly. Jesus often spoke against the Pharisees for their religious teachings and traditions. Many of the Pharisees did not like Jesus because he did not follow all of their rules. (Matthew 5:20; 23:23–36; Mark 7:1–13; Luke 18:9–14)

Preparation Day (prep-a-RAY-shun DAY) was the day before the Sabbath day. On that day the Jews prepared or got everything ready for the Sabbath. (Luke 23:54; John 19:14,31)

Prophesy (PROH-fes-sy) is to speak a prophecy, which means "message". A prophecy is God speaking through chosen people called prophets. The Old Testament has many prophecies about the Saviour who was to come into the world. Jesus was the answer to these prophecies. (Ezekiel 12:26–28; 2 Peter 1:20,21; Revelation 22:18,19) See "prophet".

Prophet (PROH-fet) means "messenger" or one who speaks for someone else. With God's help, a prophet was able to tell the people God's message correctly.

Sometimes prophets told what would happen in the future. A woman who spoke God's message was called a prophetess (2 Kings 22:14; Luke 2:36). Several books of the Old Testament were written by prophets, including Jeremiah, Amos, Jonah and Micah. (2 Kings 6:12–16; 17:12–13; Matthew 2:5,6; Luke 16:29–31; 24; 25–27; Romans 1:2; 1 Corinthians 12:28,29; 1 Peter 1:10–12)

Sabbath (SAB-uth) means "rest". It was the seventh day of the Jewish week, their day of worship to God. The Jews were not allowed to work on this day. Some Jews became angry with Jesus because he healed people on the Sabbath. They thought this was breaking the Old Testament law of the Sabbath. (Exodus 16:23–30; 20:8–11; Matthew 12:9–14; Luke 6:1–11; Acts 18:4; Colossians 2:16,17)

Samaritan (suh-MAR-ih-t'n) was a person from the area of Samaria in Palestine. Samaria was between Galilee and Judea. These people were only part Jewish, so the Jews did not accept them. They hated the Samaritans. But Jesus showed love and concern for the Samaritans. One story that Jesus told is known as the story of "the good Samaritan". (Luke 10:30–37; John 4:1–42)

Scriptures (SCRIP-churs) means "writings". They are the special writings of God's word for man. When the word Scriptures is used in the New Testament, it usually means the Old Testament. Later, it came to mean the whole Bible. (Daniel 9:2; Luke 24:27,32,45; Acts 8:32–35; 17:2,11; 2 Timothy 3:16; 2 Peter 1:20; 3:16).

Solomon's Porch (SOL-o-mon's PORCH) was a covered courtyard on the east side of the Temple. People gathered here to sell animals and exchange money. Others met to discuss the Law of Moses. (1 Kings 7:6; John 10:23; Acts 3:11; 5:12)

Son of Man was a name Jesus called himself. It showed that he was God's Son, but he was also a man. This title for Jesus comes from "one who looked like a human being" in Daniel 7:13–14. There Daniel prophesies about Jesus. (Matthew 24:30; 26:64; Mark 13:26; 14:62; Luke 21:27; 22:69)

Synagogue (SIN-uh-gog) is a Greek word that means "a meeting". By the first century, the Jews met in synagogues to read and study the Scriptures. The building was also used as the Jewish court and as a school. Both Jesus and Paul often went to the Jewish synagogues to teach and discuss the Scriptures. (Matthew 4:23; Luke 4:16,17; Acts 15:21; 17:1,10)

Temple (TEM-p'l) is a building where people worship their gods. God told the Jewish people to worship him at the Temple in Jerusalem. This temple had been built by King Solomon. It was later destroyed by the Babylonians. It was rebuilt by Zerubbabel. This Temple was destroyed by a Roman general, Pompey. Herod built a third Temple which was used in Jesus' time. (2 Chronicles 2–7; Ezra 3:10–12; Mark 11:15–17; Acts 7:47; 19:27)

The New Testament also speaks of a Christian's body as a temple. That is because God's Spirit lives in the Christian. (Acts 7:48; 19:27; 1 Corinthians 6:19)

NEW CENTURY VERSION

If you enjoyed reading this Gospel Of John and would like to read more of this translation then why not check out the full translation.

<u>Available In</u>

Hardback **0850099013**
Paperback **0850099005**

<u>Available In</u>

Hardback **0850099196**
Paperback **0850099080**

Available from your local Christian Bookshop and all good bookstores. Or in case of difficulty from:

Word Publishing
9, Holdom Avenue,
Bletchley,
Milton Keynes MK1 1QR.

Tel: (01908) 648440

For further information why not visit our website at
www.premieronline.co.uk